"Necessity may still be the mother of invention, but today's relentlessly changing world necessitates reinvention, sometimes sequential reinvention. I can think of no better guide through that daunting process than Dorie Clark's wonderfully readable and informative book."

—Robert Cialdini, author, *Influence: The Psychology of Persuasion*

Reinventing You is a must-read for anyone who wants to expand their career horizons and become more authentic—in work and in life."

—Chip Conley, author, *Emotional Equations: Simple Truths for Creating Happiness + Success;* founder, Joie de Vivre Hospitality, Inc.

Reinventing you

DEFINE
YOUR BRAND,
IMAGINE
YOUR FUTURE

Reinventing

you

DORIE CLARK

HARVARD BUSINESS REVIEW PRESS

Boston, Massachusetts

The web addresses referenced in this book were live and correct at the time of the book's publication but may be subject to change.

Library of Congress Cataloging-in-Publication Data

Clark, Dorie.
    Reinventing you : define your brand, imagine your future / Dorie Clark.
      p. cm.
  ISBN 978-1-4221-4413-8 (hardback)
  1. Career development.   2. Success in business.   I. Title.
  HF5381.C6593 2013
  650.1—dc23

                        2012034921

The paper used in this publication meets the requirements of the American National Standard for Permanence of Paper for Publications and Documents in Libraries and Archives Z39.48-1992.

ISBN: 9781422144138
eISBN: 9781422144145

For my mother, Gail Clark, with love

CONTENTS

Reinventing
you

CHAPTER 1

The New Branding Landscape

Are you where you want to be professionally? Whether you want to advance faster at your company or change jobs or even careers, one thing is clear: no one wants to spend a lifetime doing a job they hate. To succeed in today's competitive job market and build a career that leverages your unique passions and talent, it's almost certain that at some point you'll need to reinvent yourself professionally—and ensure that others recognize the powerful contribution you can make.

After all, it's clear that the era of gold watches and lifetime employment is over. How many people do you know who are lifers at a company? For better or worse, people today skip around professionally, forced by layoffs or seeking a better title or salary. Even for those who would have wanted to make a career at one company, the options are limited. Harvard Business School Professor Thomas DeLong attributes this, in part, to a precipitous decline in professional mentorship over the past several decades. As senior executives were forced to take on increased responsibilities, they stopped making time to cultivate rising talent. The result, says De-Long, is executives who "start to be suspicious about the organization and see themselves as free agents rather than saying, 'I can stay at this firm for the next thirty years.'" Rapid job turnover has now become standard.

Even if they stay with the same company or industry, professionals still need to reinvent themselves to keep up with the rapid pace of corporate change. "How are you adapting and approaching your next reinvention curve?" asks Steven Rice, the executive vice president of human resources at Silicon Valley powerhouse Juniper Networks, of job applicants. "How are you staying relevant and competitive? People have to reinvent themselves to fit into the new context of work."

Amid this new landscape of frequent job and career changing, people are increasingly working later in life. Sometimes that's due to preference, and sometimes to necessity. (Between the recession years of 2007 and 2010, the number of working Americans fifty-five and over grew by nearly 8 percent—the only group whose workforce participation rates increased.)[1] As AARP's policy director told the *National Journal,* "the resources they were counting on to retire just aren't there."[2] That means even more opportunities, or requirements, to reinvent yourself over the course of your career.

The lengthening careers of baby boomers also have an impact on their kids, millennials struggling to find their way in the workforce and hitting a wall of more experienced candidates eager for the same jobs. In 2011, the percentage of employed young people hit a sixty-year low.[3] If your early jobs don't reflect your desired future path, it's essential to be strategic about how you're positioning yourself and your experience in order to maneuver to where you want to be.

As Henry Wadsworth Longfellow noted, "we judge ourselves by what we feel capable of doing, while others judge us by what we have already done." So when you're a finance guy who moves into marketing, a venture capitalist who wants to become a career coach, or an executive trying to win a promotion to the next level, your path may make perfect sense to you, but that doesn't mean it's clear to everyone else.

Reinvention, and overcoming past perceptions, can be a daunting process. Not everyone needs to rebrand himself professionally, of course. If you do have a long-term career at your company and are happy with your trajectory, you may not need to worry about it. But for many of us, that luxury doesn't exist.

This book is intended to help executives at all stages of their careers who want something different and better in their professional lives—and know there has to be a more strategic way to do it. You may be struggling to find a toehold in an inhospitable economic climate, like Johnna, a young professional I'll profile later who was forced to bide her time with retail jobs instead of hopping on the career fast track. You may be facing a crisis in your industry that's forcing you to consider new options, like Tom, who was laid off after more than two decades as a newspaper reporter. You may, like Dan, have to fight back against misconceptions about you in order to succeed at your company. You may be looking to build new skills and explore new interests, like Karen, a corporate attorney who realized she desperately needed a change. This book is an invitation to ask what you want out of life.

When Should You Reinvent Yourself Professionally?

- You're at a new phase in life and you want to be known for something different.

- You've been laid off and need to ensure you're in the best position possible to land a new job quickly.

- You want to move up in your company, and you need to take control of your reputation.

- You've been trying to win a promotion, but feel you're being held back by misconceptions about what you're capable of.

- You'd like to move into a different area of your company, perhaps from legal to human resources, or from sales to finance.

- You're just starting out in your career and haven't built up a powerful résumé yet, so you need to find another way to stand out.

- You're changing careers and need to make a compelling case that your unusual background is an asset, not a liability.

The Perils of Reinventing Your Personal Brand

"Hi Dorie," read the message in my inbox, from an executive I'd been hoping to interview for this book. "I'd be happy to talk with you, but I'd prefer to remain anonymous. I'm afraid it might hurt my personal brand to be seen talking about my personal brand!" His message was only half-joking (I did eventually interview him), but it highlights an important truth. Again and again, as I've talked about the book in business school classrooms and corporate board-rooms across the country, I've heard from professionals who recognize the need to reinvent themselves, but still have qualms. Won't it look calculating to think too hard about my reputation? Shouldn't I just focus on doing good work?

The idea that it's somehow sleazy to manage your reputation is, of course, what the anonymous executive who e-mailed me was getting at. We can all think of examples. I know one executive who is legendary for her ability, within minutes of meeting any new person, to inform him or her that she's the graduate of two Ivy League schools, drives a BMW, and makes six figures working at a prominent firm. Sometimes, if several months have elapsed and she's forgotten she's already met you, you'll get to hear her spiel again. No one likes her.

I am in *no way* suggesting you should start spouting your credentials to passersby or puffing up your résumé. This book isn't about spin or presenting yourself as something you're not. It's not about "foghorning" your way into other people's consciousness and telling them how great you are. Instead, it's about taking control of your life and living strategically. Who do you want to be? And what do you need to do to get there? This is a book about defining your goals, working hard and ethically to get there, and then making sure that people notice once you do.

I come from the world of media relations and marketing, so I'll admit, I'm biased. But I've also seen firsthand that there are always plenty of talented, qualified people out there. If you aren't strategic about getting the word out in a thoughtful way that adds value, then other people will win the accolades instead of you.

That's why, unfortunately, it's no longer possible to sit back and count on getting noticed for your hard work alone. Years ago, the successful Wall Street investor (and former US Treasury Secretary) William Simon declared, "I have never been interested in merchandising myself or perpetuating a public image. Indeed, it is always difficult to ascertain just what your image is and it is almost impossible to improve or diminish how people view you other than through direct personal contact. I simply work hard and try to be successful at what I do."[4] Simon perfectly captures the classic upper-crust ethos that it's tacky to take an interest in anything so shallow as a mere image. And certainly, he's right that what matters are your actions and your character, rather than the spin you put on it.

But his response, which may have been perfectly appropriate for a child of the Depression who died in 2000, just as the internet era was rising, no longer makes sense for any professional who aspires to excellence. The idea that you can just keep your head down and work without any regard to office politics, for instance, has been thoroughly discredited (just look at the profusion of networking books, workshops, and seminars). Even the office wallflower knows he should hit the company holiday party or risk missing out on the connections he needs to advance. So why should it be any different for taking control of your personal brand?

Sure, you can take a chance that perhaps you'll be noticed, and perhaps all those hours slaving at your desk will pay off. But why risk it? Why not take the time to think about how you'd like to be seen in the world and then work strategically to accomplish that, rather than waiting for life to happen to you?

My Own Reinvention

I became fascinated with the topic of reinvention because I've done quite a bit of it myself. These days, I consult on strategy and marketing for clients like Google, Yale University, and the National Park Service. But my first brush with professional reinvention came shortly after graduate school, when I was working as a rookie political reporter at a weekly newspaper. It was a Monday afternoon; someone told me I should stop by the HR office before heading home that night. I figured there was an adjustment to our health insurance policy or I needed to fill out some forms. Instead, after less than a year on the job, I was laid off. As my colleagues were streaming out for the night, I had to pack up my desk and close out my online accounts; there was no chance to say goodbye.

The next morning, glancing at CNN over breakfast, I watched the planes hit the World Trade Center. I lost my reporting job on September 10, 2001, and—as the geopolitical order spun out of control and the economy collapsed—I had to figure out how to make a living, and what was next.

Over time, despite the fear and paralysis in the marketplace, I built up a stream of business as a freelance journalist. But the money wasn't great, and I was still hoping that I'd eventually be hired by the daily paper in my city. But it was under a hiring freeze, subject to the same internet-driven contraction as everyone else in the industry. For months, I plowed on, still imagining a future in journalism. So when I received an offer to "switch sides" and become the press secretary for Robert Reich, the former US Labor Secretary who was then a gubernatorial candidate, I initially said no. But an hour later, I called back; that's perhaps where my reinvention process began.

If the world hadn't intervened, I might still be a reporter; I love writing, meeting new people, and breathing the oxygen of interesting ideas. But the world is moving faster than ever, industries change, companies collapse, and sometimes our plans simply don't work out. I also would have loved to run the White House press office, but that dream died around the time the presidential candidate I later worked for lost in the primaries. To survive and thrive, you have to reinvent yourself and move on.

And sometimes, of course, your reinvention is by choice: a creative embrace of a new direction. For a couple of years, I ran a nonprofit advocacy group and could have done so for several more. Instead, I decided to become an entrepreneur and launch my consulting business, a move that's allowed me to travel the globe, consult for leading companies, and earn a great and fulfilling living.

It's easy for me to see the connections and commonalities in retrospect: how my time as a journalist enabled me to be a better spinmeister when I started working for candidates, or how running a nonprofit gave me the broad-based business skills, from IT to finance, that I needed to become a consultant. But I also know those transitions might seem random to other people (and that's not even mentioning my time as a documentary filmmaker or Harvard theology student). For years after I started my consulting business, people would still ask about campaigns I was working on, or how my advocacy work was going. Hadn't they gotten the e-newsletters announcing my new venture? Or visited my new website? *Were they just not paying attention?*

But, of course, like most people, they weren't. The truth is, the vast majority of people aren't focused on you (or me) very much. That means their perceptions are probably a few years out of date, and it's not their fault. With hundreds, or even thousands, of Facebook friends and vague social connections, we can't expect everyone to remember all the details of our lives. That's why it's so essential that we take charge of our own reinvention and ensure our personal brands reflect, to the outside world, the reality of our lives.

As a consultant who specializes in marketing and branding, once I launched my business, it was essential for me—very quickly—to practice what I preached. I had to make sure my contacts understood exactly what skills I had and what services I offered, and to demonstrate sufficient expertise that, when the right moment came, I'd be the consultant they turned to. So I honed my narrative (what am I bringing to the table?), crafted my content (so clients could get a taste of my ideas and approach), and began using every vehicle possible—from speaking to writing to enlisting "validators"—to spread the message.

That's the same process any professional goes through when reinventing herself. As I've built my consulting business, crafting marketing strategies for corporations, executives who learned about my background would often approach me. Could I help with their reinvention? Where should they start? What if they weren't sure about their destination? And how could they begin to overturn the entrenched perceptions others held about them? Over the years, I've had the pleasure of advising scores of executives looking for new directions. This book is the product of those conversations. I hope it proves useful as you consider your next professional iteration.

The Art of Reinventing Yourself

Over the course of the next ten chapters—through case studies, exercises, and research-based best practices—I'll guide you through the process.

In chapter 2—just as every business project or military operation has to begin with the facts on the ground—you have to discover how you're currently perceived. What do people make of you? What do they really respect? And what's holding you back? I'll walk through strategies and exercises to help you gain insight from your friends and coworkers so you can gather actionable intelligence without sounding nosy, entitled, or Gestapo-esque.

After that, in chapter 3, I'll turn to researching your destination. You may know you want a change in your professional life, but are unsure what that looks like. I'll lay out strategies to investigate your potential passions in the early stages, from behind-the-scenes research to informational interviews, and the right way to enlist others' help as you focus in on a new future.

In chapter 4, I'll talk about ways to test-drive your path to determine the perfect fit. You'll read about professionals who have strategically deployed volunteering, job shadowing, board membership, and more to plot their next move—and learn tips for identifying the best opportunities and ways to maximize your experience.

Chapter 5 covers how to develop and refine the skills you'll need as you reinvent yourself. How can you leverage your existing job to prepare for the one you want? Should you go back to graduate school, or is it a waste of money? We'll look at how to ascertain the most strategic, cost-efficient ways to get the knowledge you need.

Chapter 6 focuses on that elusive creature, the mentor: something everyone wants, but so few people are able to find. I'll talk about how to identify good candidates, spot unlikely gems, persuade them to help you, and get the most out of your relationship.

In chapter 7, I cover how to leverage your points of difference. Too often, outsiders will dismiss your previous experience as irrelevant. We'll show them how your diverse knowledge and skills bring something new to the table, and make you far more effective than anyone else in the room. I'll look at examples of how people can differentiate their brands and become well-known for being their best selves.

In chapter 8, I focus on creating your narrative. People want to understand who you are, so we have to craft an explanatory story that makes sense and shows continuity from your past to the present. Most importantly, we have to explain why your transition adds value to others and is an authentic extension of your true nature.

Now it's time for the big unveiling. In chapter 9, I'll discuss the nuts-and-bolts of reintroducing the new you. When's the right moment to introduce your new brand? Are there strategic opportunities you can leverage? How can you win over past friends and colleagues who know you in a different context and may question your new career identity? I'll also talk about how you can harness little-known strategies like teaming up with validators and identifying the hot spots in your company or industry where you're likely to get the most professional traction.

In chapter 10, I'll walk you through concrete ways you can demonstrate your expertise, impress the major players, and prove your worth. Every art student has a portfolio ready to be shown at a moment's notice. It's no different in the business world; no one will believe you're serious unless you begin to create content that demonstrates your expertise. That allows potential customers or employers to test-drive your approach before they make a large commitment. (If you're a graphic designer, having contacts check out an image gallery of corporate logos you've created may inspire them to send you that major new account.) I'll go over strategies such as how to leverage your online brand, affiliate with brand-name organizations in your field, get published in major journals, build credibility through assuming leadership positions, and more.

By chapter 11, you've developed a new, robust brand, and you need to stay on top of how it's perceived in the marketplace. I'll identify online channels to monitor regularly and talk about setting up your own ongoing feedback mechanisms to keep you honest. I'll talk about ways to mingle your old and new brands successfully, and the importance of staying consistent and committed moving forward. (A desire to expand into international work won't go far if you don't make the effort to learn new languages or the nuances of other cultures. And a onetime charitable gift is nice, but quickly forgotten.) The key is long-term effort, and I'll show you prominent examples of professionals who've succeeded and explain why.

Finally, in the epilogue, I'll bring it all together and summarize your road map to reinvention. As a hardworking professional, you want to understand, and shape, how you're perceived by others. By following the steps we outline in the following chapters, you're on your way to cultivating a powerful brand that reflects who you are—and want to be.

CHAPTER 2

Recognize Where You're Starting

The first step in reinventing yourself professionally is getting a handle on where you're starting. Everyone has a personal brand, whether some skeptics want to admit it or not: there's no such thing as opting out. The concept of personal branding gained currency in the late 1990s, after a famous Tom Peters cover story ran in *Fast Company* ("The Brand Called You"). But really what we're talking about is something that's always existed: your reputation. What do people think of you? What do they say when you leave the room? Understanding that, and identifying any gaps between the current reality and where you want to be in the future, is critical to beginning your reinvention process. (Even if you're not sure where you want to end up, starting with a "personal brand inventory" is useful because it can shed light on your unique strengths and areas where your colleagues think you could make a contribution.)

You may think you already know how others view you—as a skilled communicator, or an incisive numbers guy, or a manager who always brings out the best in her team. But then again, you might be surprised. One executive coach told me about a client who was shocked to hear that his colleagues considered him arrogant. Despite being a modest and fairly self-deprecating guy, his habit of interrupting people convinced them he felt superior—almost the exact opposite of the truth. This behavior, which had been hampering his career, was easy to correct once he recognized it.

The message you're giving others may be very different than what you intend. So follow the advice of angel investor Judy Robinett: "If three people tell you you're a horse, buy a saddle." In other words, listen to what those in the outside world are telling you, because they're probably right. So how do you get that feedback? There are four major ways you can get a read on how others perceive your personal brand. In this chapter, I'll teach you to become your own HR executive—or private detective—and learn how to:

- Conduct your own "360 interviews."

- Hold your own focus group with friends and colleagues.

- Examine your online presence.

- Seek out patterns in past performance evaluations or recommendation letters.

Finally, we'll integrate the data to get the full picture about your brand.

Getting Started

At the back of this book, in appendix A, you'll find "Your Professional Reinvention Self-Assessment" worksheet, which may be helpful to fill out as you reinvent yourself.

Your Personal 360 Interview

The first step when you're working with almost any corporate coach is to do a "360" (as in, all directions). Basically, that means the coach will interview everyone in your sphere—your boss, peers, subordinates, clients, suppliers—and try to elicit honest feedback about you and your performance. (It's necessary to talk to *everyone* to locate the suck-ups who are perfect in their relationships with their bosses and tyrants to everyone below.) It's obviously easier for people to speak openly to third parties who promise anonymity (coaches usually aggregate the data and won't reveal who said what). If you work for a company with a reasonable training or professional development budget, ask if it would be willing to hire an executive coach to work with you. Because many employees shy away from coaches, viewing them as "remedial education for executives," your boss is likely to be impressed with your proactive approach to self-improvement.

Even if your company won't pay for a coach, it may have recommendations about coaches you can retain personally. They can be expensive, with fees in the thousands or tens of thousands of dollars, but if you're in a position to do it, the information they gather (and their recommendations based on it) can be invaluable. You can also ask for suggestions from colleagues.

But what if you simply aren't able to work with an outside coach? Don't worry: there are steps you can take to elicit "360" information yourself. First, create a list of questions you think would be helpful in enhancing your self-knowledge. Executive coach Michael Melcher suggests "paired questions" such as, "What's my strength? What's not my strength? What career can you see me in? What career can you definitely *not* see me in?" That format, says Melcher, "gives people permission to give the full picture—they don't want to be too negative." The best questions will be the ones most relevant to you. But just for starters, some additional examples might be:

- What are three words you'd use to describe me?

- If you didn't already know what I do for a living, what would you guess?

- I'm trying to go from X to Y; what steps would you suggest for me?

- Who are some people who have some of the qualities I should be trying to build?

- What are my blind spots?

Tapping Your Network

Next, identify the people you'll be reaching out to. Whereas a coach who has been hired to interview people about you has license to talk to people in your organization, you need to be more careful if you're doing your own assessment (plus, you don't want to tip your hand if you're considering a move away from your current employer). Focus on friends, colleagues, and family members who know you well and whom you can trust to give you honest feedback (no frenemies need apply). Phyllis Stein, the former director of Radcliffe College Career Services at Harvard University, suggests identifying up to twenty people who exemplify the interests, skills, and values you admire—preferably a geographically diverse assortment of men and women in different fields—to get the broadest perspective possible.

Now, it's time to make the approach. Melcher suggests making it clear that you want to set aside time for an interview, not just regular friendly chitchat. "If you tell your friend you're interviewing them, they take it much more seriously and will give you different answers," he says. "You have to signal to people why you're having the conversation: 'I'm going to spend the next twenty minutes asking you about my brand, because I'd really like to see how I'm perceived.'"

Face-to-face interviews often yield better answers because you can follow up in real time if something isn't clear or if you'd like to probe an answer further, but they don't always work. Sometimes, geography intervenes—you're in Miami and the interviewee is in Mumbai. Sometimes, your respondent is just too busy, and the best you're going to get is an e-mail pecked out on a smartphone in between layovers. And sometimes—let's be honest—you can't handle the feedback. It's easy enough to tamp your down emotions if you're reading an e-mail; you can just snap the screen shut, take a long walk, and calm down if you see something you weren't expecting. But in real time, it can be harder to hide your emotions. Sometimes the truth can be painful, and if your poker face isn't up to snuff, you may want to stick to electronic communication.

The secret, whether you're meeting in person or sending an e-mail request, is to stress the need for honesty (otherwise, what's the point?). New York–based coach Alisa Cohn says you almost have to be forceful because friends' desire to protect you is often so strong: "Say, 'I'm trying to develop myself, and I know you love me, and I'd appreciate your candid feedback about my limitations.' And they'll say, 'You don't have any,' and you say, 'No, I'm *serious*.' You have to get them to take it seriously. You have to cajole them into it."

One trick, she says, is to provide them with leads, so they're not the one bringing up something negative: "You can say, 'I've gotten feedback in the past that I'm a tactical, not a strategic thinker. I'm wondering if you've seen that and what you think.' When you rat yourself out first, they can add on."

Arranging Your Focus Group

In addition to (or instead of) one-on-one conversations, another possibility is hosting a small group gathering. This only works if your network is geographically proximate, but the benefit is that you can leverage the wisdom of crowds when one person's idea sparks another. But instead of a Madison Avenue ad agency testing a new soda campaign or Procter & Gamble probing which scent is more "shower fresh," this is a focus group where the focus is you. Here's the setup.

Identify a group of about fifteen trusted friends and colleagues (eight to ten is the ideal number of attendees, and you know several won't be able to make it, and a few others will back out the day of the gathering). Tell them that you'd like to interview them about your brand and that you're conducting a focus group to get honest feedback because you want to grow professionally. (If you have another friend who's also interested in reinventing herself, you can suggest swapping the host duties for the focus group. You can take charge of inviting her friends and colleagues, and vice versa. That may help if you're shy; after all, it's often easier to do things for someone else, rather than yourself.)

But what if you don't have a friend you can turn to? The idea of arranging a focus group—where you're the subject of discussion—can seem hopelessly intimidating. What if your friends and colleagues consider it an imposition? (If they don't want to do it, don't worry; they'll find an excuse to beg off.) And is it really such a good idea to invite a large group of people to get together and point out your weaknesses? What if you discover that someone you respect has a negative perception of you—that you're irresponsible or unfocused, or a bad manager?

The prospect of facing a harsh truth can be daunting. But remember: your friends and colleagues wouldn't bother to participate if they didn't care about you and value you. Everyone has strengths and weaknesses, and your posse is coming together because they want to help you become as successful as possible. Indeed, regardless of whether you hold a focus group, these are likely the people you're going to need to rely on in your personal reinvention. Why not involve them in the process now and get their support? They're your best hope of honest feedback about your strengths and weaknesses, how you're currently perceived, and other intelligence that can save you time and energy in identifying your path forward. Even more importantly, they're your allies—the ones you'll turn to for mentoring, feedback, and (eventually) new business and referrals. It may seem like an imposition to reach out, but the truth is, it takes a village to reinvent yourself.

Making It Work

Instead of a focus group facility—they're very fancy, usually located in nondescript office parks or skyscrapers, and have conference rooms with a mirrored wall so the client can observe everything from a darkened room—your living room will probably have to suffice. Make sure you have enough comfortable chairs and, just as in real focus groups, bribe people with dinner and/or copious, high-quality snacks. Order plenty. Real focus groups also generally pay participants $50–$100 for a few hours' work, but your friends are doing it as a favor to you. (However, if you're able, it's still a classy gesture to give a small token of your appreciation, like a gift card for coffee or a bookstore.)

Because these folks are participating in your focus group out of the goodness of their hearts, don't abuse it. Keep the length to ninety minutes and be strict about timing. Allow thirty minutes up front as a cushion for late arrivals, and for people to mingle and snack. Then you've got sixty minutes to probe the questions you most want answers to—how you're perceived, your strengths and weaknesses, what kind of jobs or environments people can most see you in, and so on. Two roles are critical here: the facilitator and the scribe. If you're a terrific moderator—you can keep meetings going efficiently, shut ramblers up politely, probe interesting statements—then go for it. But for most people, it's tricky to handle, especially when the subject is you. Instead, tap a friend or coworker you think excels in this area (whose meetings do you actually enjoy going to?), and see if they'd be willing to help.

A good role for you if you're not facilitating is to be the scribe. Sit silently in the back, don't interrupt, and just take notes on what people are saying. Write down anything that seems interesting or important (it's also a good idea, with permission, to record the session so you can play it back and review it in the future). You may want to interrupt or argue, depending on what's said, but your job is to stay quiet. Instead, work out an arrangement in advance with the moderator so you can slip him notes with questions and he can follow up on any key points.

You may also want to build in five minutes at the end of the session and request that attendees write down a short summary of their perceptions (three words that describe you, the most important skill you should work on developing, and so on). Some participants, despite your entreaties, may be too shy to verbalize their thoughts, so this is a good way to ensure you've captured their insights.

Arranging your own focus group takes work, and it's not for everyone. But it can yield interesting insights rapidly and get allies on your side as you prepare to rebrand.

Try This

- Make a list of the fifteen people you're going to invite to your focus group.
- What are the most important questions you want to ask? (Aim for four to six.)
- Who's your moderator?

Mary's Focus Group

Mary Skelton Roberts had built an international career as a conflict resolution expert.[1] But eight years ago, she found herself back in the United States looking for a new challenge. "I felt like I had given conflict resolution all I had and it was time to explore something else," she recalls. She mentioned her quest to her friend Don, who floated the idea of a personal focus group. When Don offered to run one for Mary, she immediately agreed.

He suggested she invite participants "who knew me really well and could speak about me in different phases of my life," Mary recalls. So she developed a list of ten names: her "dream team" of friends and advisers who would provide honest feedback, ranging from childhood friends to college buddies, and from professional colleagues to siblings.

Though some might have felt trepidation about inviting colleagues to analyze and evaluate them, Mary didn't hesitate: "My friends already give me feedback and advice, so even if it isn't usually this scripted, I already have that kind of relationship with the people I approached. Also, people said that one of my biggest strengths was the ability to listen and give thoughtful feedback, so some may have viewed it as an opportunity to reciprocate and help me out." All ten agreed to come.

They sat in her living room, plied with snacks, and began filling out four worksheets Don distributed. The top of the worksheets were labeled:

- Mary's Greatest Gifts Are . . .
- I Could See Mary . . .
- The World Would Be a Better Place If Mary . . .
- I Will Help Mary by . . .

For several hours, Don led the conversation, asking participants to share their responses for each question. Mary sat silently, taking it in. "All I could do was listen," she says. "I was able to ask clarifying questions or ask for more information, but it was in the spirit of taking it in, not responding or critiquing."

Mary found the process revelatory. Other people "almost have a bird's-eye view, and they can see your life in ways you may not be able to, because you're involved in day-to-day living." The participants praised her communication and leadership skills, and urged her to think broadly about how to translate them: "They could see me working for a political campaign or writing a children's book." (Mary is now a senior program officer at a major foundation.)

The session focused on strengths, not weaknesses. But Mary nonetheless picked up important clues from the conversation. "There was a sense among people that I was a highly creative person and should be doing more in that space," she says. "My interpretation of that is that I can be very intellectual, and maybe there should be more of a balance with creativity."

Perhaps the most startling insights were about her personal life: "It was the first time somebody said out loud, 'I want to see you with a child; I think you should explore it.' Up until that point, I wasn't sure I wanted to have kids, but that comment made it more relevant for me, and something I should be thinking about more carefully."

After the session, she sat down with her professional coach and developed a six-month and yearlong plan following up on the insights and advice she'd received, from increasing her connections to other consultants to doing more work locally. The focus group, says Mary, "took me to the next level in terms of my professional development. It helped me refocus my consulting practice to include more training and development, which I loved doing and was really good at." But the most important change was personal. A year and a half later, her daughter was born.

Your Online Presence

These days, a major part of your personal brand is online. Sure, your friends and colleagues' perceptions are based on your day-to-day interactions, but if you have even minor celebrity (you blog for an industry website) or you're job hunting (and people are doing basic background checks), the broader world is forming its image of you courtesy of Facebook and Google. Your first step? Reviewing—and controlling—your online paper trail, because if you don't do it first, it may come back to haunt you.

In fact, the *New York Times* profiled a company called Social Intelligence, which "scrapes the internet for everything prospective employees may have said or done online in the past seven years" and assembles a dossier on the candidate.[2] It has ferreted out racist remarks, drug references, sexually explicit material, and weapons fetishists. Hopefully that's not your shtick. But even if you're not a gunrunner or trolling for OxyContin on Craigslist (like one job candidate Social Intelligence reviewed), you still may not be in the clear.

Your online presence may be spit-polished, with only your wise quotations in industry journals and incisive blog posts about the future of business. Then again, you may not appear online exactly as you'd like to be perceived. Your plight may be banal—you're a fanatical runner and the only thing that comes up is your race times. It may be your parents' fault (if your name is Joe Smith, search engine optimization is a cruel joke). It may be someone else's fault (one guy I know was plagued first by sharing the same name as a former MTV Asia VJ and later a congressman forced to resign due to a sex scandal).

But sometimes the picture that emerges is downright frightening, as was the case with a young woman I once met with as a favor to a friend. She was obviously smart, just finishing graduate school at an Ivy League university and looking for a position in marketing. We had a good chat, but at the end of the meeting, she leaned in and lowered her eyes. "There's something else I should mention," she said. "I'm not sure if you Googled me before we met, but . . . there are some negative things being said about me online."

It turns out she had a deranged ex-boyfriend who was posting defamatory things about her online. Because of her distinctive name, his rants littered any online search—and made her life and job search very difficult (she was pursuing legal action). Of course, the fulminations of a jilted ex shouldn't be part of your personal brand. But thanks to the internet, even the most private of matters can quickly attach to your public persona.[3]

Don't Stop at Facebook

Review everything, because companies like Social Intelligence will. They report that less than a third of the content they dredge up comes from major sites like Facebook or Twitter. Instead, they trawl lesser-known spaces, where it may feel "safer" to post—and lead candidates to mistakes. Comments on old blog posts, bulletin boards, Craigslist ads, or old Yahoo! Groups archives are all targets, not to mention photos and videos (which may have been uploaded by friends with poorer judgment than your own).

In addition to your first pass, you may want to have someone else review the data as well. Everyone knows a picture of

---

Try This

- Search for yourself not just on Google, but also on other search engines such as Bing and membership sites (that may have various privacy settings) like Facebook.

- Search for your name in quotation marks—as in "Dorie Clark"—so you'll only find hits with that exact phrase. (Otherwise, you may turn up any document, however long, that happens to have both words in it.) Don't forget to search for variations of your name, including common misspellings or nicknames.

- Don't give up too soon. Scroll through every page, because you may find a smoking gun on page twenty-six of your Google search. If something malicious, false, or inappropriate is out there, someone's going to find it eventually, and for your sake, it better be you.

---

you with a bong is probably ill advised. But some people might feel that membership in a "This Is America—I Shouldn't Have to Press 1 for English" Facebook group is witty, while others could see it as racist. (Yes, that was a real case vetted by Social Intelligence.) Getting another perspective can help you discover blind spots and areas where your idea of "just a joke" could be badly misinterpreted.

Seek Out Patterns in Past Performance

You may also have access to hard data about how others perceive you, namely, performance reviews from your job (or previous ones). Not every employer has its act together enough to require formal sit-downs and evaluations, so don't worry if it's just not available. But especially in larger organizations, you're likely to have a paper trail. (If you've applied to graduate programs or for specific fellowships, you may also have access to recommendation letters others have written for you, which are a treasure trove of intelligence.)

First, gather the material, and then take a step back. You're going to have opinions about everyone who's written a word about you. Maybe your former boss claimed you were fanatically detail-oriented, but you only acted that way because she was so disorganized; nothing would have gotten done if you hadn't taken the reins. Maybe your grad school professor criticized you for being late on a few assignments, but didn't take into account that your dad was diagnosed with cancer that semester.

It's natural to get defensive when you see yourself evaluated on paper and attempt to justify any criticisms. Try not to. We're not concerned with one person's hobbyhorse issue ("Jeff is a great employee, but he keeps confusing 'there' with 'their' in his memos!"). It's when everyone (or almost everyone) says your spelling, your micromanaging, or your lateness is a problem that you should take it seriously, and do the same with your strengths. (Stein, the former Radcliffe career counselor, observes that her clients are often keenly aware of their weaknesses, and find it much harder to appreciate their positive attributes.)

Are You Too Likable?

One caveat is to be aware of the "likability conundrum." Harvard Business School Professor Amy Cuddy notes that many people view warmth and competence as "inversely related"—

that is, if you're very nice, you must be a little dumb.[4] That's bad news for female executives, who are often stereotyped as, and culturally trained to be, extremely warm.

Indeed, a study in a psychology journal revealed that in performance evaluations of junior attorneys at a Wall Street law firm, "technical competence was more heavily weighted in men's numerical ratings," as compared to interpersonal warmth for the female attorneys.[5] Thus, while the women were lauded much more effusively in the comments section, the men received higher overall numerical ratings (and you can guess which was given more weight in determining promotions).

I remember once overhearing a reference interview for a woman named Kelly, whose former boss praised her as "a wonderful girl" with a "terrific personality" and who was a "delight to work with." It was clear the boss thought highly of Kelly and wanted to help her win this coveted new job. But at the end of the interview, Kelly sounded very nice—and very weak. No man would ever be described in those terms, and if she were up against a male candidate whose reference instead praised his "extraordinary competence" and "passion for winning," I was pretty sure I knew who'd get the job.

So be on the lookout for stereotypes that may crop up. They may or may not be accurate (every woman isn't warm, every Frenchman isn't aloof, every gay man isn't witty), but they're probably shaping how others view you.

Bring It Together

Finally, synthesize your data. Any high-quality pollster strives to get a representative sample (if you have too many senior citizens or not enough Hispanics in the pool, your result can be dramatically skewed). Similarly, be sure you're assigning the appropriate weight to each variable; rather than obsessing about something one person mentioned, you're looking for patterns. It's easy for something negative to stick in your craw (one friend has quoted a critical review of her work to me so many times that I can recite it verbatim, and it was written a decade ago). But the power of one harsh appraisal can cloud your understanding of how you're perceived in general. Remember: you're looking for patterns and trends.

Ask yourself the following questions, and make sure you're taking into account every category—360 interviews, your focus group, your online presence, and performance reviews and recommendation letters:

- What adjectives—both positive and negative—do people use to describe me?

- What skills do they say I have—or lack?

- What aspects about me or my brand are most frequently talked about?

- Are any aspects of me or my brand cited as unique or unusual?

Now, most importantly, you have to determine whether you like what you hear. Begin to think about what words you *want* people to link you with. Notes Cohn, "Maybe people say, 'I see you as thoughtful, methodical, and nice.' Those are lovely professional qualities, but it's not a leadership brand like 'decisive.' It's not bad, but it's not going to get you to the C-suite." Our job in the next chapter is to help you identify where you want to go—whether it's the C-suite of your current company or into a new field altogether—and begin to reshape your brand to get there.

REMEMBER:

- ✓ If three people say you're a horse, buy a saddle. In other words, whether or not you believe a perception about you is true, if enough people share it, you'd better take it seriously.

- ✓ Personal focus groups with friends and colleagues can reveal telling insights about you. Think seriously about organizing a gathering or at least approaching trusted colleagues individually to get their perspective.

- ✓ Make it safe for others to give feedback that's real. If you can tell they're sugarcoating, beg them for the truth and ask paired questions that let them talk about a strength and a weakness.

- ✓ Google yourself, and don't stop on the first page of search engine results. Check to make sure there are no smoking guns or false information about you online. (If there are, contact the site administrator and nicely ask for it to be removed. If he stonewalls, you may eventually need to involve a lawyer.)

- ✓ Don't give too much credence to outlying opinions; instead, watch for patterns.

CHAPTER 3

Research Your Destination

Now that you have a better grasp of your current brand and the strengths and weaknesses that go along with it, it's time to research your next move. If you already have a working theory (I want to transition from project management to sales), you can test and investigate it before diving in. And if you're still unsure what's next, this is your chance to spark ideas and gather new insights so you can better evaluate opportunities down the road.

One caveat is that, at this point in your reinvention, it's often a good idea to keep a low profile. Later on, once you've solidified your brand, you'll want to shout it from the rooftops (that's how you can win clients for your new business or get a plum job offer where you can utilize your new skills). But at this early stage, you may not have a fully formed sense of where you're going, and that uncertainty has the potential to confuse others.

As San Francisco–based executive coach Rebecca Zucker notes, "if you're not sure what's next, you still need to come across in a way that inspires confidence and makes other people want to help you. You can't go out into the world lost, because no one will want to spend social capital on your behalf." The secret, instead, is to slow down and determine where you really want to invest your energy.

In this chapter, we'll talk about ways to crystallize your future direction. We'll cover:

- Why you may need to take time off first

- How to conduct behind-the-scenes research

- How to win friends and not alienate people through informational interviews

Take a Break

If you're been suffering through an unsatisfying job or career, you may be eager to get on with the rest of your life. That was certainly the case for one woman who visited Phyllis Stein, the career counselor. "She'd been a solo veterinarian for fourteen years," recalls Stein, "and she was on call seven days a week for those fourteen years. I literally had never met anyone in my life who had worked like that, not even doctors and lawyers." The woman was miserable; when Stein asked about her career aspirations, her first words were, "I don't ever want to see another animal again." She wanted to start planning her next move, but Stein insisted she wait: "I said, 'I don't think you should even try to figure out what you're going to do next. You should go away for nine months of vacation, to make up for the vacations you didn't have in fourteen years, and you can come back next September.' She was in a burned-out condition where creative thinking just wasn't possible."

Sure enough, when the woman returned the following year, she was simultaneously more relaxed and more focused. "She very quickly found a new direction for herself that was incredibly creative," says Stein, becoming an international public health veterinarian, which allowed her to travel the world helping animals.

Your Behind-the-Scenes Research

In the pre-internet dark ages, it was almost impossible to decipher nontraditional career trajectories. *How did she get a job like that? What kind of training did he have?* Unless you knew them personally or were a reporter and could badger someone for a bio and press kit, you'd never know. Needless to say, some of the most exciting jobs don't have a clear path.

But things are different these days. In the post-Google era, you can make massive research headway before even talking to a live person. I know one successful executive who's made a habit of "stalking the biographies" of people he admires. The best way to get where they are, he decided, was to emulate them—exactly. From becoming a White House Fellow to developing a taste for marathons, he matched their regimen for success. Obsessive, yes, but he's barely into his thirties, widely lauded in the media, and has already raised over $1 million for charity with his running.

Reading is, of course, another main research channel. You can take a page from Bill Gates who, as described by Steven

Johnson in his excellent *Where Good Ideas Come From,* takes two weeklong "reading vacations" each year, where he plunges into the stack he's been collecting. So save up your list of titles (from friends' recommendations, reviews in industry magazines, or Amazon's algorithms) and make sure you're conversant with the leading books in your field before you start networking with people.

There are four immediate benefits. First, particularly if you're diving into biographies or memoirs, you can get a better sense of whether or not a given field is for you (Michael Lewis's *Liar's Poker,* for instance, has given generations a taste of life on Wall Street). Second, your immersion will help you master the terminology; the jargon thicket can be dense in some fields, and you'll want to sound credible. Third, you may pick up some fun anecdotes to share as you're schmoozing, which can help you grease the wheels of social interaction.

Finally, you'll be able to ask better, more-informed questions once you start meeting with other professionals to talk about your goals. Stein tells her clients, "If one of the things they're exploring is being a lawyer, I don't want them going to a lawyer and asking a dumb question like 'What's it like to be a lawyer?'" Executive coach Michael Melcher agrees: "You want to show that you've done your homework—that you've taken it as far as possible before talking with the person," and urges people to consider the "highest and best use" of the person they're interviewing. In other words, if you can find out certain information online or through books, don't waste a professional's time with it. You want to ask the person more sophisticated, refined questions (instead of "Where can I go for training?" think "I'd like your advice on choosing between two different revenue models").

Try This

- Make a list of the people you think are doing the most interesting things (anyone from famous business leaders to your neighbor who lived in Bangkok for a year).

- Stalk their bios online. You can usually find them on the "about" page of their company's website, but you may also have to do some detective work. If they're well-known, read news articles to familiarize yourself with their career progression.

- Identify patterns. If every person you admire is a Rotarian, maybe you should think about joining. If they all raise money to fight breast cancer, you can build a solid network by pitching in.

- Brainstorm a tentative list of goals, based on your idols. You can refine them later (and we'll work together to figure out the "how"). But now's the time to think big: visiting at least fifty countries, getting your own radio talk show, raising a million dollars for charity, being named partner, or whatever most appeals to you.

Informational Interviews

Armed with your behind-the-scenes research, you're finally ready to talk shop with actual experts. Informational interviews are an unbeatable opportunity to network with people who are doing what you want to do, to ask real-time questions about what their profession is like, and to weed out bad choices. (Friends of friends and your alumni network are usually the best starting places for people to meet with.)

Karen Landolt, a corporate attorney who transitioned to running a university career services office, requires her students to conduct at least four informational interviews and report back on them. She recalls, "I'd have people come to me and say, 'I want to work at Goldman Sachs,' and I'd say, 'Great, who have you talked to there?' They'd say no one, but they make a lot of money. And I'd say 'Yes, but they work 120 hours a week—and have you talked to anyone at 3 a.m.?'"

There's a risk to informational interviews, however, that most people don't recognize: if you don't know how to do them well, you can torpedo the relationship if you don't make a good first impression. Here are six steps to follow.

Step 1: Be Clear about the Help You're Asking For

As a favor to friends, I'll sometimes do informational interviews with folks they know who are breaking into the workforce or looking to change jobs. The people are generally delightful, and I'd love to help them, but many are so vague that I honestly don't know how. When you need a job and aren't totally sure what you want, it can seem like a good strategy to leave yourself open to fate. "I'd like something in communications." Well, yes . . . but what kind of communications job? Marketing? Advertising? Public relations? For a nonprofit? A big corporation? In health care? Consumer products? It becomes a monumental task to even think about how to provide assistance.

It's far easier to help people with specific, targeted requests. Francine, who took a marketing class I taught at Tufts University, asked for advice on getting "a job in marketing for a food-related business." Thanks to her specificity, it was immediately apparent how I could help. I set her up with informational interviews with my friend Stephen, a restaurant consultant, and Larry, who ran an artisanal chocolate company. She ended up helping Larry with some product demonstrations and he connected her with an internship.

But what if you aren't sure what you want or you're interested in multiple potential careers? *Just make something up for now*. Being specific will expand your options, not limit them. People are likely to say, "I don't know anyone in New England archaeology, but if you like historic preservation, I know someone who works at the Victorian Society." You want to paint a picture so clear that your contacts are thinking about real-life people they know who can help you.

Finally, a caveat—you're likely to hurt your cause if your informational interview is actually a bait and switch. Don't call up your contacts for a casual get-together, only to surprise them with the news that you, too, want to get into their field. Instead, be up front about your motives and they'll likely say yes.

Step 2: Respect the Fact That They're Doing You a Favor

Let's face it: you're the one asking for someone else's time, so you want to make it very convenient for him. Let him pick the date, time, and location, and be sure to pay for his drink or meal. (I've heard some friends who are unemployed grouse about spending money taking out folks who are earning a healthy paycheck, which is exactly the wrong perspective. Their hourly rate is probably high enough that it's costing them hundreds of dollars in lost productivity to meet with you. The least you can do is buy them a damn cup of coffee.)

You also want be sure you're not misusing their generosity by taking too much time. Says Landolt, who estimates she's done well over a hundred informational interviews in the past decade, "If they say they have twenty minutes, I'll keep track. I'll say, 'It's been twenty minutes, and if you have more time, I have more questions, but if not, I want to respect your time.'"

Step 3: Ask the Right Questions

Here's the wrong one: do you have any jobs for me? Because if they don't, it'll shut down the discussion permanently. Good questions reflect a basic understanding of the field (you're not bothering them with banal questions) and focus on their lived experience, so you can get a sense of what their job is really like. Stein suggests questions like:

- What is your typical day like? Typical week? (And if there's no such thing, ask them to describe the most recent.)

- What do you like most and least about your job?

- What does it take to be successful in this field? In this company?

- What is the average salary range at this level?

- I'm planning the following steps toward obtaining a job in this field (name them). Have I overlooked any strategy or resource you think might be helpful?

Step 4: Leave with Other Names

You can learn from salespeople here: be sure to ask if there are other people in the company or in the field they think you should connect with, and would they be willing to make an introduction? LinkedIn is also helpful here, because you can easily see if your colleagues have connections to, for example, other marketers, Comcast employees, or specialists in Argentinean culture. And don't forget alumni networks, whether they're from college, grad school, or former employers.

Recalls Landolt, "When I was making a transition, I was at a huge firm with 450 attorneys and a turnover rate of about 70 percent. There were attorneys all over who had worked there, and I used the network, because we'd been through the same war. We didn't know each other, but I'd talk to current employees at the firm and ask, 'Can you introduce us?' And they'd say sure."

Try This

- Write down your one-sentence positioning statement that you can share with others. (If you have multiple possible goals, create one for each.) An example might be, "I'm exploring a transition from intellectual property law to entertainment law," or "I'd like to learn more about how others have handled moving from manager to vice president, and what skills are necessary."

- Spend an hour at a bookstore (online or real-world) searching for titles that intrigue you. Make a list of at least a half-dozen books you plan to read. Buy them now, or request them from the library.

- Write down a list of ten people you'll ask for an informational interview. E-mail three of them right now.

- Make a list of the five to ten questions you intend to ask, so you can get the maximum value from your informational interview. Don't forget to include questions that help you learn more about the person as an individual, so you can identify ways to stay in touch and possibly help them in the future.

Step 5: Keep the Connection Alive

Write your thank you note; it does make an impact. Elizabeth Amini, an online entrepreneur, recalls that after one informational interview, "a year later, when I went into that office, my thank you note was pinned to the wall." But, while most people treat informational interviews as stepping stones to job leads or onetime data infusions, the real goal is turning a thirty-minute meeting over coffee into a relationship. One of my favorite business books from the 1980s is Harvey Mackay's *Swim with the Sharks Without Being Eaten Alive*. Mackay ran an envelope company—the ultimate commodity business—yet was able to prosper by differentiating his firm through great service. He mandated that his employees use "The Mackay 66," a list of questions that they should answer about their customers, not through a onetime interrogation, but by getting to know them over time.

During your informational interview, in addition to facts about a person's job, you ideally want to form the building blocks of an ongoing relationship by finding out key details you can follow up on. Maybe they're just back from a vacation to Fiji, or you both like the Dodgers, or your kids went to the same school. That's your starting point, so make a point of sending them interesting travel articles, shooting them a note when their team makes the playoffs, or inviting them to sit with you at the school fund-raiser. With each interaction, strive to learn more about them so your relationship becomes more three-dimensional. The process of learning someone's hometown, college, names and ages of children, favorite hobbies, favorite restaurants, previous jobs, and long-range goals provides a raft of opportunities to connect with her over shared interests and keep up a dialogue.

Step 6: Master the Follow-Up

Just as your contacts are helping you, you want to try to add value to their lives. Maybe it's offering to introduce them to someone else you've met who's also originally from Boise or Berlin or Beijing. Maybe it's providing them with a helpful connection (one friend who asked for my assistance in preparing for a job interview seriously impressed me with her networking chops when she later connected me with a prominent business contact she'd met at church). And maybe it's just being an encouraging voice. I try to make a point of congratulating colleagues when I see they've been quoted in a magazine or the local business journal.

Another great excuse to keep in touch with your contacts is integral to the "viral" nature of your informational interviews. After you've met with someone, be sure to follow up with her—and the original person who referred you to her. Says Rebecca Zucker, the executive coach, "I always encourage people to go back to the people who were interviewed and thank them, and let them know, 'Here are some of the things I learned, and I'd love to talk more with you as I progress'—make it an open feedback channel. You can tell them, 'Here are two to three things I'm going to be working on.'"

Elizabeth Amini agrees. "The easiest thing is to be in touch around major milestones," she says. You can send holiday greetings ("thank you for your mentorship this year"), updates on advice they gave you, and relevant articles (Elizabeth, while connecting with venture capitalists, put out Google Alerts on the companies they were backing and sent them interesting clips). Sometimes opportunities to connect simply present themselves. In the wake of the 2004 Asian tsunami, Elizabeth made a small, $10 donation in the name of each of her mentors and sent them a short note letting them know. "It wasn't calculated at all," she says, "but I got the most responses ever. People were so thankful."

Conducting a slew of informational interviews might sound stressful, but key to enjoying the process is keeping it in perspective: "I like having lunch with people," says Karen Landolt. When she felt demoralized in her job as a corporate lawyer, "it would give me something to look forward to. It was almost therapeutic, and how I got through my days: at least I get to have lunch with this interesting person."

Making Connections You Never Thought Were Possible—Elizabeth's Story

Elizabeth Amini thought she wanted to be a surgeon. But after finishing college with a cognitive science degree, she discovered during a hospital internship that medicine was a bad fit. After starting a graphic design firm and later working for NASA, Amini found herself, at thirty, unsure of her direction. "I felt really lost," she recalls. "All my friends who were also pre-med had graduated from medical school and were practicing, and here I was, not knowing what career direction I should take."

She vowed to use a strategic approach to find her calling. She made a list of possible professions that intrigued her and set out to obtain five to ten data points, such as informational interviews, for each one. The problem? She didn't have many contacts in her target fields, so she had to get creative about succeeding through cold calls.

First, she'd search online to find the right person to talk to at each target company (she had identified large companies based in her city through online research). She'd type in the name of the company along with a phrase like "international business vice president" in order to get the right name. Then, she'd check the date (to make sure it was a current role and he or she hadn't been promoted or left the company) and try to glean some salient information (for instance, that the executive was heading up an expansion into South America).

Next, she'd look up the company's press office or investor relations department online to find the e-mail address of the contact person, which would allow her to deduce the company's standard e-mail pattern (for instance, john.doe@company.com). She'd also continue to dig to learn about the executive's preferred nickname. "When the name is Michael," she says, "search on the web to see if they go by 'Michael' or 'Mike.' Otherwise, the secretary is going to think, 'Nobody calls him that; you probably don't know him,'" Finally, she'd call the main company line after hours to get the voice-mail directory in order to learn the executive's voice-mail extension.

Armed with this information, she was finally ready to make her move. She could e-mail or, even better, call directly. "When you call and ask for an extension number directly, they never question why you're calling the way they do if you ask for someone by name," she says. Also, she recommends calling just before or just after business hours, when secretaries are unlikely to be at their desks, but hardworking executives may be around. "It's important to realize the secretary is there to screen you out, so you want to avoid the secretary as much as possible," she says.

It would have been easy for her to target low-ranking employees. But Elizabeth resisted the impulse. "Everybody tells you to start with people you know, one or two degrees of separation," she says. "But chances are the people you know are in middle management, or maybe just a few years out of university." If you really want to get to know what an industry's like, you have to talk to seasoned veterans.

The CEO—the public face of the company—is bombarded with requests. That's why Elizabeth started her initial research one notch lower, with the office of the chief operating officer, "because that secretary knows everybody," she says. Her goal wasn't actually to score an interview with the COO, which was probably unlikely. Instead, it was to get his imprimatur: "You can say, I know the COO is probably not the right person to talk to, but who is your best salesperson, or your rock-star marketing person? And then you can say the COO's office recommended them, and they're not going to blow you off."

Elizabeth learned quickly that the typical request (thirty or sixty minutes of someone's time) was usually rejected. Busy executives aren't going to crack open their calendar for someone they have no real connection to. Instead, she would warm them up with context, letting them know the COO's office recommended them and that she had read about them online.

Says Elizabeth, "If they have a book, read it, because *no one* writes to these people and says, 'I read your book.'" Then tell them, "I was impressed by XYZ, and I'd like to ask you some questions about how you became so successful. Is it possible to schedule a ten-minute phone call?

Or, if you're free, I'd be happy to take you to lunch." Most people will opt for the phone call, which seems easy in comparison to lunch, and now you have an appointment on the books.

Another crucial point is timing. Most professionals' schedules are heavily booked for the next few weeks, so Elizabeth discovered if you ask for a calendar slot "in the next week or two," you're likely to get turned down. Meanwhile, asking to connect with them "sometime this year" won't seem urgent and, even if they agree, may result in an eventual brush-off. Elizabeth suggests the best time frame to request may be "this month or next," because there are likely to be unscheduled blocks still available.

Elizabeth often had to persevere through blow-offs or rejections. "One guy said I needed to talk to someone more junior, so I said, 'I'd like insight from the most successful person in the department, and that's you.'" That line won him over. Another person, in real estate development, screamed at her and said, "I don't have time to talk to some [#*$@ student; I'm up to my neck in lawsuits!" and hung up on her.

Says Elizabeth, "To me, that's a data point. I got the same information as I would have in a ten-minute interview." Another executive literally canceled on her six times ("there was a pole vaulting championship, the kids were sick, he was traveling," Elizabeth recalls), but she kept calling back. "Until I get a 'No, never call me again,' this is in play," she says. They eventually met.

Finally, she learned you have to be willing to say yes to opportunity. Browsing the *Forbes* 500, she read about a billionaire real estate mogul who lived in her city. She called after 5:30 p.m. (post-secretary hours), got him on the phone, "and, oddly, he agreed to lunch," she recalls. She was thrilled with the opportunity, but shortly after she got off the phone, she panicked. "I said 'Pick your favorite place,' but then I thought, where do billionaires go for lunch? What if lunch is $1,000?" She decided to proceed, despite the risks: "I'll put it on my credit card," she thought, "and if it's more than my rent, I'll find a way to pay it off." The mogul took her to a local deli (his favorite spot) and lunch for two came to $17. He spent an incredible ninety minutes with her and "outlined exactly what it took to be him."

Elizabeth's informational interviews gave her insights that continue to resonate in her new career, running an online game start-up based on cutting-edge brain research. "You end up with all these random lessons that are important, even if the person's field is not relevant to you in the end," she says.

REMEMBER:

✓ If you're unsure of your future destination, you might need some time off first. It can be hard to think creatively if you're burned out.

✓ Start researching your prospective job or industry behind the scenes before you connect with people live. Get conversant with the major blogs, and read popular books that people in the field will be familiar with. You'll want to be ready to meet them and have a sophisticated conversation about the industry.

✓ Once you set up a meeting with someone, research them online. Check LinkedIn so you're aware of mutual connections (beyond the person who introduced you), and identify other commonalities or aspects worth commenting on (you once worked at the same company, or they're on the board of a charity you support).

✓ Be on time for your informational interview. If you arrive late, you've not only wasted their time, you've also missed your opportunity to buy their coffee or meal, a double faux pas.

✓ Put a reminder in your calendar to follow up with the people you're meeting with: first, to thank them right away; next, a week or two later, to offer some kind of value (sending them an article you thought they'd like, and so on); and then four to six weeks later, to update them on your search and let them know how you're using their advice.

CHAPTER 4

Test-Drive Your Path

At this point, you've researched your new path thoroughly, both behind the scenes and through informational interviews. You probably have a much better sense of what areas interest you (consulting and venture capital sound intriguing), and what potential pitfalls might lurk (I'm interested in moving up to senior vice president, but can I live with the travel requirements?). Now's the time for your immersion experience.

It's impossible to know if you'll really like a new career direction until you try it out. To avoid costly mistakes—and wasting your energy—you can take a short-term test-drive. In this chapter, you'll read about professionals who kickstarted their professional reinventions with a variety of exploratory techniques, including:

- Apprenticing

- Volunteering

- Job shadowing

Plus, we'll cover:

- How much time and money can you spend?

- Dreaming big

- The path isn't always linear

Apprenticing

When Joanne Chang graduated from Harvard in 1991, she'd been virtually swept into her first job. As a math and economics major, "it seemed natural to go into investment banking or management consulting. In fact, they were really the only two options Career Services offered. There were big presentations on campus," she recalls. "Everybody would go to them and sign up for interviews; everybody tried to get in on it." When a blue-chip management consulting firm offered her a job, she grabbed it.

But two years later, much of it spent on the road advising companies spanning every industry from insurance to telecom, she knew it wasn't her calling. "There wasn't an immediate sense of accomplishment," she says. "I'd take part in big projects and there was a fair amount of busy work. I'd think, 'this isn't helping the client.'" She'd always been interested in cooking (at Harvard, she'd become known as "the chocolate chip cookie girl") and decided to give it a try. "I sent a bunch of letters to chefs in town that I didn't know, but I knew their reputation," she says. "I said, 'I have no formal training, but I love cooking and I'm interested in getting into the restaurant world, and I'll take any position.'"

Impressed with her chutzpah, intrigued by her résumé, and short an employee who had just left, Boston power chef

Lydia Shire called Chang literally the next day and invited her for an interview. She got the job and started as "a bottom-of-the-ladder prep cook," tutored by a sous chef who "trained me, showed me recipes and what I needed to do: how to set up the station, what the dishes should look like." After three months, she worked her way up to her first job as a line cook.

The transition wasn't always easy. "It's grimy, hard, physical labor," she says. "It can be mundane, and there's a lot of stress." But she soon realized the food industry was where she wanted to be: "I remember clearly telling one of my consulting friends how exciting it was to be surrounded by people who were passionate about their work. When you cook, you're not making any money, so when you do it, it's people who are there because they love cooking." And unlike the spreadsheets she created as a consultant, her work in the kitchen had a direct impact: "You make a terrine, you slice it up, put it on a plate, and the server comes back and says they loved the terrine. It was an immediate gratification I hadn't had up to that point in my career."

Today, Chang is the impresario behind Flour, a chain of three acclaimed bakeries in the Boston area, and the co-owner (with husband Christopher Myers) of the upscale Asian restaurant Myers+Chang. Now she's on the other side of the equation, hiring (as Lydia Shire did) people of all ages wanting to break into the restaurant industry, and she's more convinced than ever that apprenticeships are critical. She says:

> There are misconceptions about what it's like to be
> in the food business. Many people want to reinvent
> themselves in this industry without a real understanding

of what it's like because of what they witnessed on Food TV or from going to restaurants or bakeries. But if you're going to make a big change in your life, it's imperative to spend some time working in the field before making a jump—you know, "I used to be a doctor but I love to cook, so now I'm going to be a chef."

I've seen so many people come to work for us as career changers and after a year or two, they say, 'Wow, it's not what I want to do.' It's a business and people have to recognize that. I think it can be dangerous to take a hobby and make it into a career, because it's not always fun. This isn't home where you can make a cake and if it's not that great, people still love it because you made them a cake. Here, people pay money and I don't know them—so they're not going to give us the benefit of the doubt.

Volunteering to Build Experience

At the time of her career transition, Joanne was young and single, and she was willing to take a low-wage job in order to learn new skills. It's a great path if you can afford it. But even if you can't, volunteering on nights and weekends provides an opportunity for any professional to build skills and get a taste of new possibilities.

Rebecca Zucker, the San Francisco–based executive coach, says of volunteering, "It allows you to network with a new group of people in your target area, it helps you to keep your skill set fresh or build a new skill set, it's something you can put on a résumé—and it shows your commitment to a particular path." She recalls one client who wanted to explore clean tech, a popular industry in Silicon Valley that was hard to break into without previous experience. "He volunteered to do research for a private equity firm in a certain niche within clean tech," she recounts. "Not only did he learn a ton and have something to put on his résumé, it was instrumental in helping him get a job in the field."

Volunteering can be beneficial even within your own company, because it allows you the opportunity to meet new people and expand their perception of you. New York–based executive coach Alisa Cohn suggests stepping up for committees that will allow you to broaden your contacts and build connections with people in different departments: "You could volunteer for the diversity committee, or the company picnic. You can volunteer for any press function or global committee. It might feel thankless, but what you're getting is a broader network and the experience of doing something different. It's especially good if you feel like you've been boxed in or pigeonholed. If you're in engineering or finance and want to get more experience in marketing or strategic planning to expand your skills, they can't stop you because you're volunteering."

Joining a Board

One of the best ways for professionals to broaden their résumés is to join a nonprofit board. That was certainly Karin Turer's experience. As a junior-level staffer at an organization for the homeless, it never occurred to her to join the board of directors of another nonprofit, until a friend told her about an opening at MassBike, the statewide bicycling advocacy group. "My friend said, 'You're biking all the time, you should do this,' and I thought it sounded great," said Karin. "I sort of saw it as my civic duty, that if I'm going to be biking a lot, I should be involved to make it better."

At first, serving on the board just seemed like a fun way to pursue her passions. She'd been to a bike event in Maine and thought MassBike should replicate it as a fund-raiser. When the board agreed, she was delighted. "I went into it assuming there would be a lot of other people helping out with the event," she recalls. But the truth about small, understaffed organizations slowly hit her: "It really turned out it was just me." With her reputation (and the organization's) on the line, she went into overdrive to ensure the event's success. "It was absolutely insane," she says. "I created and directed all the aspects. We designed and planned ten ride routes, we solicited sponsorships, did the publicity, communicated with the police and town officials and got the permitting, and did volunteer recruitment and management."

The event—best known for the "Pie Race" Karin designed, featuring a timed race that measured riders' alacrity both on their bikes and in wolfing down pie slices—became a fund-raising hit for MassBike, running successfully for five years and drawing up to 350 participants a year. (In one of my career iterations, I served as MassBike's executive director for two years and got to watch Karin's work up close.) The Bike Festival, which raised tens of thousands of dollars, served as Karin's "sweat equity" on the board, which required members to either donate or raise money. The event had a big impact on MassBike's bottom line, but it had an even bigger one on Karin's professional life.

Thanks in large part to her work on the Bike Festival, Karin realized she loved event planning and fund-raising.

On the strength of her board experience, she was hired for a development job at a local college and now, years later, has her own fund-raising and event consulting business. Without her board service, she says, it wouldn't have been possible.

"When you have a day job, you have to color inside the lines," she says. "There's a general idea of how you're going to do your job, and people have certain expectations. But the freeing thing about being on a board is if you have an idea, unless there's some reason it's horrible, they'll say, 'Great, run with it.' You get to try out things you don't in your day job. You have more freedom to try things that are riskier or may not work. And then you can take those skills back to your day job. I always felt it was a real asset to whatever I was doing Monday–Friday to have board stuff I had done in my back pocket."

Hitting the Campaign Trail

Volunteering and apprenticing aren't just useful tools for young professionals, however. Deborah Shah earned her MBA in the late 1970s and spent three decades building a successful, lucrative corporate career. "I didn't have to work," she realized a few years ago. But she also didn't want to retire. What should she do with her life?

She traveled to Rwanda, Haiti, and Cambodia to explore her interest in microfinance, but nothing stuck. All that changed, however, when she heard a candidate for governor speak and felt a connection. She'd always enjoyed politics, but strictly as an observer: "I would typically watch the morning shows on Sunday and read the morning paper. I knew what was going on in the world, but not as an insider."

She decided to get involved and showed up at headquarters, where they gave her the most basic grunt work: making phone calls to voters. But she earned trust and greater responsibility because "I was the phone banker who showed up every day." Eventually, the campaign asked her to organize a senate district, then another, and she finally became regional field director. She worked on the campaign for eleven months, unpaid, but in the process she discovered a passion: "I was interested in persuading people to vote. I really liked campaigning."

After the campaign ended, she learned something else: she'd made a name for herself. A state representative she'd met on the trail was headed for a special election and wanted her to run his campaign. When she helped him win, other calls poured in. In the past five years, she's headed races for governor, state senate, and city council, plus a US Senate campaign. "People have different phases in their lives," says Deborah. "The work I did for thirty years was extremely meaningful and satisfying, and so is this."

Job Shadowing

Apprenticing and volunteering are important short-term ways to learn about interests and try out new fields. But you may not even need that level of commitment. Occasionally, a day is all it takes. One coach recalls a web designer client who "liked design but couldn't stand spending five days a week in front of the computer." Looking for a creative career that had more interaction with people, she became interested in floral design and read about it extensively. She did ten informational interviews in the field and, convinced it was right for her, agreed to her coach's suggestion to shadow someone for a day.

"At the end of the morning," the coach recalled, "she had three questions: Is the room always cold? Is the floor always cement? And are you always on your feet? And the guy said, 'The room is always cold because we have to keep the flowers fresh, the floor is cement because I'm dropping wet flowers on it, and I'm always on my feet because we're moving around and delivering flowers.' And that was the end of that."

For those whose dream jobs aren't located nearby, there's VocationVacations, a company founded in 2003 that allows participants to test-drive over 125 new careers. Say you'd like to be an alpaca rancher. If yes, and you don't know any personally, you can pay $849 and head off to Oregon for a two-day apprenticeship with a real-life ranch mentor. If you'd prefer to become a schooner captain, plunk down a grand and (during the June–September sailing season) you can join your mentor for one-on-one instruction roaming the coast of Rockport, Maine.

If you want to make any kind of a professional leap, even if it's to something less esoteric, like becoming a freelance writer, it's essential to do your "personal and professional due diligence," says company founder Brian Kurth. "It's doing your homework and getting questions answered that you didn't know you needed to ask," he says. "One question I always have clients ask mentors is 'What do you know now that you didn't know when you launched your business?' The goal is for the clients not to make the same mistakes—to hit the road faster, quicker."

For clients who can't take time off or aren't yet ready to spend a few thousand dollars on their adventure, Kurth's company offers phone and Skype mentorship at lower rates. And sometimes the greatest benefit of a VocationVacation is simply its ability to reassure others. Kurth recalls a recent client who was "a very active photographer—he was so skilled, he was actually a photography instructor." He didn't need to learn any new camera techniques, but he did need to convince his wife he wouldn't ruin their nest egg by moving into photography full-time. "His wife said, 'It's great you want to start your own photography firm,'" Kurth recalls. "'And it's not that I don't trust you, but I want you to better understand the business side.' So she took the VocationVacation with him." As you reinvent yourself professionally, sometimes the most important thing is having your team behind you.

Try This

- Make a list of dream companies or individuals you'd like to work for. Now go on LinkedIn and see who you know who works there or may be able to provide an introduction.

- Create a list of the value you could potentially provide. Include a range—from stuff anybody could do (making phone calls to voters, pushing paper in the mailroom) to your unique talents (copywriting to improve their fund-raising letters, programming to create a new app for them).

- Think about how the opportunity can best fit into your life. Can you take time off for a concerted internship? Could you get a sense of what you need to know in only a day or a few days? Or can you keep your professional life steady but build new skills incrementally with a board membership?

- Put it on your calendar. In the next month, reach out to your target organizations—ideally through a contact, but cold-calling if need be—with your proposal for how you can help.

How Much Time and Money Can You Spend?

If you have a lot of interests, it can be hard to know where to begin to look for your own path-testing opportunities. First, ask yourself how much time you're able to commit, and how long you need to see if a given path is for you. My friend Robbie arranged to take every Friday off from his fundraising job for several months, so he could devote the time to expanding his nascent consulting practice. It was a low-risk strategy that enabled him to test demand and establish a foothold.

If you want to become an alpaca rancher, however, and you currently live in a metropolis, your free Fridays aren't going to help much. But spending time in the country—or, if finances permit, a trip with VocationVacations—may give you enough insight to see if you want to pursue it further. In general, a few days are sufficient to eliminate possibilities, but not enough to set a life's course. So if you fall hard for the alpacas on your first date, make sure to take a couple weeks' vacation on a farm, or maybe even schedule several months' sabbatical, before buying a herd.

Dreaming Big

When you're determining the best place to get your professional experience, however, don't let your existing contacts dictate your future. If you can turn up something interesting, that's great. But if not, don't hesitate to dream big and seek out your own opportunities. That's what Joanne Chang did when she wrote unsolicited letters to her culinary idols (perhaps intrigued by her unusual background, *every single one of them* eventually wrote back). The truth is, because so many people limit themselves, there's often not a lot of competition at the top. If there's a senior executive at your firm you really admire, reach out and see if he'll agree to be shadowed for a day. Unless you're writing to the worldwide CEO, there's probably little demand and he'll be flattered.

Pluck will get you everywhere. A couple of years ago, I met Kevin Roose, then still an undergrad, who had already published a book (*The Unlikely Disciple,* about his time "undercover" at conservative Liberty University, learning the ways of evangelicals). Kevin, who went on to become a *New York Times* business reporter, had landed his big break by interning for A. J. Jacobs, an editor at *Esquire* magazine. And how did he win this coveted position?

A. J. tells the story in his book *The Year of Living Biblically* (his own religious experiment, in which he tried to follow the Bible literally): "Day 237. I got an unexpected email today. It arrived in my in-box at 1:07 p.m. from a guy named Kevin Roose. 'Allow me to introduce myself. I'm an eighteen-year-old native Ohioan in the middle of my first year at Brown.' Kevin went on to explain that he's going to be working at a café in New York this summer, but he wants to be a writer, and he noticed I went to Brown as well, and . . . would I be willing to take him on as a part-time personal intern?"

The rest is clearly history. As Kevin's experience proves, it's often easier to create your own opportunities. A. J. Jacobs probably would have been inundated with résumés if he'd posted an internship notice with Brown Career Services, but Kevin, by asking for what he wanted in a strategic and targeted fashion, was able to evade the hordes.

The Path Isn't Always Linear

Finally, you may have to tamp down your inner critic. Sometimes finding the right career path can mean turning your back on expensive training, like Karen Landolt's law degree, and sometimes it means a loss of security. Joanne Chang recalls her parents' reaction when she abandoned management consulting: "Nowadays, there's a glamorized view of the food business. But in 1993, if there was a Food Network, nobody was watching it. They said, 'You're giving up a really stable, secure, financially lucrative career that's going to take care of you. It comes with health insurance, vacations, a 401(k), cabs to take you home when you work late. And restaurants have no health insurance, you're paid hourly, and when you leave, no cab takes you home. Are you sure you want to do this?'"

Then there was the prestige question. "People were like, 'Really? Is that what you're going to do?'" recalls Chang. "It's essentially blue-collar work, and I was coming from a background where most, if not all, of my peers were working in nice, cushy white-collar jobs. It's not that people considered it a step down—but it doesn't have a clear path."

Getting the most from your experience means going into it with an open mind and a sense of possibility. Sometimes you'll learn the most by applying your training (a senior executive could do an operations analysis for her favorite nonprofit), but other times, the best learning experience may involve starting at the bottom. "I've never been concerned about what I'm doing as long as I'm feeling useful," says Deborah Shah. "Years ago, I'd go with my daughter and we'd do 'Adopt a Pet' care, and you'd be cleaning out cages.

Who cares? You're trying to help out." She credits her experience as an entrepreneur. "I was always a person who was willing to do whatever it took," she says. "Running your own company, you're a jack of all trades; you book your own travel. I'm not a snob about work, and if what needs to happen now is we're all going to fold letters and stuff them into envelopes, you do it."

My mom took a similar approach when she decided—in her early sixties—to become a barber, despite having a PhD and a successful counseling career. "It was actually fun to tell people I was going to barber school," she says. "They'd say, 'Why are you doing that?' and it would spark a great conversation. I never felt embarrassed—I had the education—but it was a way to connect with people." She now cuts hair for most of her friends, and me.

The secret is realizing that sometimes the path isn't linear. Says Susan Leeds, a longtime investment banker who shifted into the energy efficiency field, you have to "accept the fact that sometimes you have to take one step back to take three or four steps forward. It would be incorrect if I said I made a lateral shift: I went *backward*. But because of the benefit of my years of professional experience in a competitive field, even though I went back, I was able to move forward fast— to leapfrog forward."

REMEMBER:

✓ Start by evaluating how much time you can spend on test-driving your path and whether you'll need to earn money while doing so. That will help you determine the right way to proceed. If you only require a minimal salary, you can try apprenticing full-time, as Joanne did. If you need to continue with your current full-time job, consider other ways to build your skills, like joining a board or volunteering on the weekends.

✓ Job shadowing can be a powerful way to see what someone's professional life is like. Most leaders, unless they're at the C-level, usually aren't deluged with requests. If you develop a thoughtful request that explains why you'd like to learn from them in particular, they may well say yes.

✓ Make it clear, when you're taking on an apprenticeship or volunteer assignment, that you're willing to work hard. No one wants to take a chance on someone who thinks they're too good for the dirty work.

✓ The juiciest volunteer and internship opportunities often aren't advertised, so identify your own targets and approach them.

✓ The path isn't always linear. Don't be discouraged if you temporarily have to go backward in terms of salary or prestige in order to prepare yourself for your next career leap.

CHAPTER 5

Develop the Skills You Need

Apprenticing, volunteering, and job shadowing are all great ways to immerse yourself as you investigate new ways to advance or change your career. But there's another crucial strategy: leveraging your current job to cultivate the skills you need for the future. In some cases, that means expanding the contours of your current job so that it encompasses new challenges, and in others, it's about providing a secure base that enables you to explore new outposts safely. In this chapter, you'll learn about:

- Ensuring your job grows with you

- Strategic moonlighting

- When to go back to school

- When not to go back to school

- Targeted strategies to build your skills

Ensure Your Job Grows with You

For nearly twenty years, Richard worked as a high-powered reporter, first covering the oil industry, then electricity deregulation, and eventually government securities. An economics major in college, he thrived on the tight deadlines and arcane subject matter: "The type of reporting I do is statistics-based," he says. "It's made a big difference that I understand the nitty-gritty of market relationships and how they work."

But after so long in the trenches, Richard felt this once-coveted position had become tiring. And that's why, to Richard's surprise, his job satisfaction and professional success flourished when he took on a new assignment three years ago. "The company decided they wanted lifestyle coverage," he says. "They were going to do food and wine, and I said, 'Can I start writing?'"

Richard isn't interested in tracking trendy ingredients or celebrity chefs. As a seasoned business reporter, what he cares about is "the economic and sociological perspective" behind America's culinary obsessions. His eyes light up when he discusses one of his favorite pieces, a behind-the-scenes look at the "command center" of a major food festival, where—for almost seventy-two consecutive hours—restaurateurs dish out nearly a half-million servings of gourmet dishes.

He still spends about 85 percent of his time reporting on government securities, but it's the dash of culinary coverage that inspires him most. "All veteran journalists are looking for ways to stimulate themselves by writing outside their beat," he says, and he's convinced it makes him a better writer. Covering securities, "I have to be so analytical, I have to digest information so quickly, and there's such a rapid turnover of stories. But with a food and wine story, I can sit back and think about what language I'll use. The style is a lot different, so it makes me feel I'm using all parts of my brain if I'm able to do both."

His new beat has also given him an unexpected leg up in covering securities. "The business sources like to chat with me because they know I'm different than other reporters," he says. "It gets me more of an 'in.' They'll say, 'I have a client coming into town; what do you recommend?' Entertaining out-of-towners is a big thing, and I have some level of authority, so it makes them feel more confident."

Richard's not looking to go into food writing full-time. His bosses are encouraging, he says, but caution him to "remember what your real job is." And that's fine with him, because he's found a way to mix his interests and create a fulfilling job. As we parted after a morning interview, I asked what he was working on that day. "Two stories," said Richard. "One's about whether Europe's economy is going to blow up, and the other is about grilling on a budget."

Strategic Moonlighting

Richard found a satisfying way to expand the scope of his day job, giving him a taste of variety and a chance to develop new writing skills. Patricia Fripp, now a well-regarded professional speaker, took a slightly different path when she moved to San Francisco from her native

England in the 1970s "to find fame and fortune." Trained as a hairdresser, Fripp soon discovered she possessed special skills; slowly and strategically, she leveraged them into a new career.

Her first skill was relentless hustle. "In those days, you were selling the concept of having your hair styled," she recalls. "It was more expensive than going to the barbershop, so you were not just selling the idea of 'I'm the best hairstylist'; you were selling the idea that you should spend three times more on your haircut, but I managed to get them in." She cajoled customers to provide referrals, and when business was slow, she'd call them up: "John, it's six weeks since your last haircut, and you're going to look shabby." She'd hit executive watering holes after work, and flirt and pass out business cards; instead of taking a lunch hour, she'd fit in extra clients who only had time to come during their own lunch breaks.

In short order, she'd developed a clientele of powerful Bay Area professionals from major companies like Levi Strauss and Wells Fargo, and eventually launched her own salon. And she made good use of her time with them. "When I had people sitting in my chair, I'd say to people in the public relations business, 'If you had a small hairstyling salon, how would you promote it?' Or I'd ask what made you the best salesperson in your company, or what did you do in your company that prompted a big company to want to buy it? I'd say to other stylists, 'Why would you talk drivel when you have the most interesting people in your chair?' You take advantage of having interesting people in front of you who know more than you in certain areas."

Her second skill was her easy command of a room. Patricia had begun doing hair product demonstrations. When her executive clients discovered her sideline, "they said, 'Go speak to my Rotary,' or 'I have a staff meeting; do you want to give a speech on customer service?'" Eventually, as referrals built, her free talks became paid ones. She was thirty-two years old when she realized she might want to make speaking her career, but she was also only two years into a ten-year lease for her salon: "I was smart enough to realize that becoming a professional speaker is a long-term goal; you don't just quit your job. You plan your divorce; you don't just leave."

So she bided her time and reinvested her profits: "I was one of the first people in the speaking business with fancy press kits and demo videos, because I could put all the money I was making by speaking back into the business, because I had another business to support it." She also spared no expense honing her craft, hiring speech coaches, and taking classes in comedy and screenwriting to hone her storytelling abilities. She even hired a choreographer to evaluate her physical movements and use of the stage. (Recalls Patricia, "He said, 'You use the width well, but now you need to use the depth,' and that was worth paying him for.")

In 1984, a little less than a decade after giving her first paid speeches, Patricia sold her hairstyling business and became a full-time speaker. "At that point, I'd built my speaking career and had more than replaced my income from the salon," she says. "There comes a point where you need to focus 100 percent of your attention on what you're doing. I wanted to focus on the next area."

Patricia leveraged her initial hairstyling career in several crucial ways. First, she made connections with key corporate executives—initially her clients for hairdressing, and later for speaking. Second, she sharpened her communication skills, first by talking to audiences about hair products, and later moving on to business themes. And finally, she strategically reinvested her salon profits, enabling her to build up a robust speaking career prior to going full-time.

When to Go Back to School

Richard convinced his bosses to expand his beat into food and wine. Patricia nurtured her day job, while steadily growing her expertise. But what if the skills you need just can't be obtained by moonlighting or taking on new job responsibilities? It may be time to go back to school for additional training.

Heather Rothenberg knew she wanted to change the world. A sociology major, as one of her first jobs out of college, she ran a small nonprofit helping to revitalize an economically depressed neighborhood. "I became fascinated by the link between transportation and people," she says, and decided she wanted to become a transportation safety specialist—but she didn't have any of the necessary training. She quickly realized she had to go back to school. "To some extent, I was a little oblivious to the skepticism," she recalls. "If I'm going to do something, I'm going to find a way to do it. There were people when I started the program who said, 'she'll never make it.'" Heather slogged through calculus, physics, and engineering classes; those were all undergraduate prerequisites to make up, before even starting her doctoral program.

Going back to school, especially in a technical program where she had the least math and science background of anyone, wasn't easy, but humility was key. "I didn't shy away from taking on things I knew would be harder for me than for other people," says Heather. "When we were working on group projects, I was willing to put in the extra time, ask around for help on my own, read the extra books, and do what I needed to do to hold up my end of the deal, rather than passing it off. I was really willing to ask for help and to acknowledge that I had different experiences. Maybe I wasn't as familiar with the software, but if I could find someone who was willing to spend an extra half-hour to help, I wasn't shy and really expressed appreciation." When she finished her doctorate, Heather had competing job offers; today, she works in Washington, DC, at her dream job as a transportation safety analyst.

Heather's experience illustrates the best reason to head back to graduate school, that is, when it's essentially mandatory. That's the case if you want to move into a job that requires specific technical training (like transportation engineering) or professional licensure, such as becoming a doctor or lawyer or acupuncturist. Another valid reason is when you want to expand your skills and networks, and feel ready to get the most out of the experience.

Alice Denison's dream since childhood was to become a painter. She grew up in Queens, close enough to witness the ferment of the Manhattan art scene, but never to consider it a real possibility for herself. "I was raised to believe art was a hobby," she says. She studied it in college, but needed a job and plunged into the work world after graduation. "A lot of people in creative pursuits face a marginal existence," she says, "and I knew I'd be a nervous wreck if I didn't have health insurance."

She became a nonprofit fund-raiser and over the next fifteen years worked her way up to chief of staff, eventually following her boss into a prestigious job in state government. All the while, inspired by the working moms around her, she pursued her art: "If they're getting up at all hours to raise a child, I can find the time to advance my work." She began rising before 5 a.m. to paint for three to four hours before work, and realized how much happier it made her. But she could also be hard on herself: "If I overslept until 5:15 and got to the studio at 5:30, I felt like I had failed. It was just crushing."

During those years, she applied twice to master of fine arts graduate programs and was turned down. But in 2005—a full twenty-five years after finishing college with her art degree—she tried again and got accepted to a part-time program at the Fine Arts Work Center in Provincetown, the Cape Cod, Massachusetts, art mecca. She was determined to get the most out of it: "I was old enough to be very blunt and fearless with the questions I'd ask. I think it really hit me that getting my work to a place where I felt good about it, having a chance to get it out there, getting to be respected— that's what success is to me."

At times, as an executive very much outside the New York art scene, she questioned whether her painting would be taken seriously. But she reminded herself, "The starving artist in the garret is a convention, and artists break conventions all the time. Look at Wallace Stevens, who was an insurance salesman. You can find examples of people who've done bizarre things to feed themselves and keep the lights on."

But in her graduate program, Alice found someone who did believe in her work. Years before, she'd met a prominent Boston art professor when she'd taken classes with him. They reconnected when he was a visiting artist in Provincetown, and he loved her work. Says Alice, "He told me, 'If I can help, get in touch.' And I said sure, but then he came back into the room and said, 'I mean it.' If he hadn't come back into the room, I wouldn't have done it." But she got up the courage to create a wish list of Boston galleries she'd like to represent her. With her professor's help, Alice's first choice said yes.

For Alice, who was committed to taking her skills to the next level and needed to make more contacts in the art world (which she couldn't do from within the confines of her day job), going back to graduate school was the right answer. But, even though it's often marketed as a professional panacea, for many people it's not.

When Not to Go Back to School

I often get inquiries from executives looking for advice about whether they should go to graduate school. They feel like their career is stalled, and wonder if an MBA, a JD, a doctorate in organizational psychology, or maybe a journalism degree would give them that extra edge. It's true that top-tier programs can provide valuable networking and connections (and I wouldn't advise anyone to turn down the opportunity to attend Harvard Business School or one of its elite peers).

But unless we're talking about the pinnacle of top schools, my answer is generally no. As someone who has a great but perfectly useless (in the professional world) degree in theology, I have firsthand knowledge that a master's degree doesn't win you extra points or gain you any additional respect. *It's your demonstrated expertise—not your academic credentials—that counts in the business world.*

Unless you *have* to go back to grad school, as in Heather's case, you should think carefully about your end goals, especially when nearly $100,000 in debt is likely to be involved. You may be interested in the subject and want to expand your worldview. You may have a clear sense of particular skills you want to develop, as Alice did. You may want to wait out a recession and learn something new, which is better than moping around unemployed. But a lot of graduate programs are simply a racket, preying on people's status concerns and fears about the future. In many cases, it's simply not worth it.

You can often learn what you need and make connections with professionals in your field, rather than fellow newbie students, through networking, volunteering, or other inexpensive means. Given the massive cost involved, it's often better to rule out every other option first and return to grad school only when you've determined it's the sole route to meeting your personal objectives. Something as simple as starting a blog can sometimes be a much more potent demonstration to employers that you know what you're doing.

Try This

- What skills do you need to develop for your rebranding?
- Can you learn them on the job or through a side venture, or do you need to return to school?
- Make a list of three things you can do in the next several months to enhance your knowledge base (take an adult education class, seek out a new assignment, connect with knowledgeable colleagues, create your own research project, and so on).

Do a "Mini-MBA"

Dave Cutler decided to take a hybrid approach during his recent job search. A husband and father, he knew he couldn't afford to take a year or two off for full-time studies. But because he wanted to land a position in social media, a new area for him, he decided to go all out demonstrating his skills and simultaneously pursue additional studies. Dave honed his personal blog to showcase his knowledge of social media. He developed a "Hire Dave Cutler" website and began actively using a variety of social channels. Finally, he entered a weeklong "Mini-MBA" program at Rutgers.

"With things you learn by doing, there are going to be gaps in your knowledge," says Dave. "I wanted to fill in those gaps and have more of a foundation in social media, as well as something tangible to point to, because it's hard to call yourself a social media guy without something on your résumé." The program was ideal because it was taught by knowledgeable, real-world practitioners, some of whom Dave already followed on Twitter.

He left with practical tips (one professor suggested he place a QR code on his résumé, which has increased his "scan-through" rate) and some valuable connections, including a link to a guest lecturer who is the business partner of the influential blogger Chris Brogan. Thanks to the connection, Brogan took up the "Hire Dave Cutler" cause and has repeatedly plugged him on his weekly web TV show. In general, says Dave, the mini-MBA course "isn't a substitute for work experience. But it says I've made a concerted effort to learn about and understand this business."

Targeted Strategies to Build Your Skills

Depending on your goals, the best recipe may be targeted classes that focus on a particular skill. Joel Gagne completed all the courses for a master of arts in government. But in the midst of running a company, a couple of cross-country moves, and a new baby, completing his master's thesis just didn't seem that relevant. "I don't want to say those classes were worthless, because they weren't," he says. "There were one or two nuggets. But as far as directly affecting my professional life, graduate work has not had the type of impact necessary or given me the business skill set I need."

Instead, he's made a point to continue his professional development by taking targeted classes that address clear business needs. "Let's take writing," he says. "I don't need the fundamentals. I need to be skilled at how to write a blog post, or how to write a proposal—specific things that will impact my work. Tackling something small and more focused has served me far better than completing that master's degree or anything I took from studying for it."

He's taken classes on goal setting, effective business writing, and how to sell your business. He took a noncredit class at the University of Chicago on creative writing, but with an emphasis on business applications. "Almost no one in the room was looking to write the next great novel," he recalls. "Everyone said, 'I'm in business, I need to be able to write better; my work can't sound clunky or dry. I have to capture someone's attention off the bat: how do I do that?'"

As you reinvent yourself professionally, you'll need to cultivate new skills. But you don't necessarily need to pony up for an expensive graduate degree. Think carefully about your goals, and you may be able to obtain the experience you need through volunteering (as we discussed in the last chapter), expanding the parameters of your current job, moonlighting, or taking targeted classes to expand your skill set.

REMEMBER:

✓ You can often push the boundaries of your current job in ways that allow you to explore new avenues and build new skills. Ask if there are relevant new responsibilities you can take on.

✓ Going back to graduate school shouldn't be your default option. If it's not mandatory for your chosen field, think hard about whether the debt and time out of the workforce is worth it. The most prestigious

schools have powerful brand value and alumni networks that can turbocharge your career, but that's not
the case for most programs. Ask yourself if there are
other, cheaper ways you can obtain the knowledge
you want.

✓ Create a concrete list of skills and knowledge you
should develop. That'll force you to think harder about
your education. If you need to be able to write better
reports, you can probably find targeted help (such as a
class or a writing tutor), rather than jumping into a
two-year program that only tangentially touches on
what you want to learn.

CHAPTER 6

Who's Your Mentor?

At this point, you've identified your new path, tested it out, and begun to develop the new skills you need to succeed. But, regardless of your abilities, entering a new field or working your way up the corporate ladder can still be a confusing, frustrating process. It helps to have an experienced guide to help you navigate. But mentors, sadly, are in short supply. While it would be great to have a sage senior professional tap you out of the blue ("I recognize your potential—let me help you achieve it!"), it's probably not going to happen. Though some people get lucky, for most of us, mentors never materialize.

But that doesn't mean you can't still benefit from their wisdom. The secret that most people don't realize is that you have to seek them out, and they often come in unexpected packages. In this chapter, we'll cover the eight steps of building successful mentor relationships, including:

- Discovering who you want to emulate

- Ensuring they're a good fit

- Identifying the right mentor for you

- Learning from the wisdom of crowds

- Learning what your mentor, uniquely, can teach you

- Developing your own curriculum

- Making it worthwhile for your mentor

- Giving back

Step 1: Discover Whom You Want to Emulate

Years ago, Joel Gagne (the executive mentioned in chapter 5 who took targeted professional development classes) was elected to the school committee in his hometown—the youngest member in town history. That's when he met Steve, the owner of a public relations firm and a longtime committee member thirty years his senior. "I was impressed by Steve's ability to take an emotional, complex problem and very eloquently break it down," Joel says. "He could ask questions and give an opinion that I might not agree with, but he did it in a way that people could understand. Having that patience and maturity, that was something I very much lacked when I was twenty-six years old. He was a mature, respected professional. That's what I saw in Steve that I wanted people to see in me."

Steve and Joel's mentor relationship is classic—an older statesman helping a young protégé. But think broadly: don't assume your mentors have to be older, or in the same industry. You can sometimes learn the most from unexpected sources. Hank Phillippi Ryan is an Emmy Award–winning

TV reporter in Boston, famous for righting wrongs with her "Hank Investigates" segments. But after decades in the news business, she found herself inspired to take a new path by, of all people, her intern.

"There was a wonderful young woman who worked at my station," she recalls. The intern dreamed of returning to Boston to become Hank's full-time producer, and after a few years paying her dues in other TV markets, a job eventually opened up. "She was about twenty-seven and had written a book," says Hank. "She was really a kid. She was writing a romance novel and asked me to edit it, so I did, with much delight. I was immersed in my off hours editing her novel and it was percolating in my head: *if she can write a book, I can write a book*. It's a Zen thing: when the student is ready, the teacher will appear."

Step 2: Ensure Mentors Are a Good Fit

Not everyone will be a great mentor, so it's important to learn as much as you can about that person before pursuing or investing in a mentor relationship. David is a medical school professor and heads the emergency department at a prestigious hospital. Medicine is a field theoretically based on learning over time from more senior doctors. But the process doesn't always go smoothly. "I've sometimes had people coming to me after they've struck out with someone who would more naturally be their mentor," he says, "because that mentor was focused on what he or she thought the trainee should be doing and didn't take the time to figure out what they actually wanted out of their career. Good mentors should listen to what a mentee is saying and help them figure out what they want for themselves, rather than having a set idea and pushing them to actualize that plan."

At David's rarefied institution, there's an emphasis on going into academia or public policy; if the newly minted doctors realize they're not interested in that path, the pressure can be enormous. "I try to start the conversation with a gentle statement: you've spent your whole life trying to please other people, your parents, then your college professors and your medical school professors. Now you don't have to answer to anyone's dream. It's about your own dream, and once we figure it out, I'll help you achieve that. They feel much more relaxed after that conversation; they don't feel like they're letting somebody down."

Another prospective mentor warning sign is an inability to make time for the mentee. Says David:

One of the flaws I see in some folks who consider themselves mentors is they're too busy, or they give the appearance of being too busy. If a resident or junior faculty member asks to see me and I don't make them feel like it's something I want to do, it's hard for them to ask again. So I try to make it one of my highest priorities. It's not that I'm not busy—but successful mentors make you feel it's something they're eager to do, rather than a favor you're doing for the person. There's always something else you can do with your time, something that will fill up your CV rather than talking with someone about a potential job or a tough case last week that's making them upset. But if you're available over time to talk with people, you build up a relationship that can be really rewarding.

So follow David's advice: make sure your prospective mentor is willing to make time for you and has your interests (not their own agenda) at heart.

Step 3: Identify the Right Mentor for You

Joel and Steve built their mentor relationship through shared work on the school committee. But what if a good mentor relationship just isn't happening for you organically? Sometimes you may have to take a more deliberate approach.

Roxy Kriete recently retired after a successful career in nonprofit management. But she began as an elementary school English teacher at a small private school. "We had zero money, and the classrooms were overcrowded," she recalls. "A tiny house came up for sale next to the school and everyone wanted to buy it, but there was no money." She'd helped out in admissions for the school, though, and knew one family that she thought might have the resources to help.

So on a Friday, as the staff was sitting around brainstorming about how to find 120 small-ticket donors, she had a brainstorm: "I said, 'What if I could go get it from one person by Monday?' They said 'Ha, ha,' and bet me a six-pack of Sam Adams that I couldn't. I called the family up and talked to them. It turned out the guy was the grandson of people who had founded some big steel company in Pittsburgh. They had a huge amount of family money and they were grateful to the school, so I got it. The school made me a half-time development director, and now I had to figure out how to do the job."

She didn't know anyone she could turn to for advice, so she started attending meetings for a group called Women in

Development. When she found out they had a mentor program, she immediately signed up and was paired with Sally, a longtime fund-raiser for a premier liberal arts college—an experience that was "lifesaving" for navigating her new job.

But, sometimes, a formal mentorship program doesn't seem right or isn't available. If you have a casual relationship with someone who seems as if she could be a good mentor, executive coach Michael Melcher suggests that "it can be a very powerful thing to tell somebody you want them to be your mentor," as long as you explain what you mean (so they can determine whether it makes sense for them).

Melcher recalls, "I did this ballsy thing once that I'm really proud of: I know this mover-and-shaker guy, and I worked on a project with him eight or nine years ago. He's a captain of industry, but I think he sees me as a different, youthful version of himself. I said, 'Dick, I'm going to ask you a question: I want you to be my mentor, and what that means is every six months we'll meet for breakfast and you give me advice.' And he said, 'Of course.' The key is I *asked* and I *explained* what the role should be."

Step 4: Learn from the Wisdom of Crowds

At times, of course, there may not be one perfect person to be your mentor. Instead, you can focus on creating a broad-based "personal board of directors," with members who have different skill sets and are willing to advise you in smaller, more discrete ways. (Napoleon Hill popularized a variation of the concept in *Think and Grow Rich* as "Mastermind Groups.") When she first started her business, executive coach Alisa Cohn participated in a group that called themselves the "Buzz

Club" because they'd promote each other and ensure account-ability. "We were all women entrepreneurs around the same age, and we met for coffee monthly," she recalls. "I could bring anything to them and bounce it off them. They can be better strategic thinkers about you because they can show you a por-trait of yourself."

In putting together your group, don't just tap the people who know you best, says Cohn. "It's about who you think would have the most insight—people you instinctively trust. It's nice to have old friends and colleagues, but it can be equally helpful to have new people on your team because they see you now, and aren't hindered by baggage of you from fifteen years ago." A fellow member ran a networking group, Cohn recalls, "and at the time, I was nervous about public speaking. She said, 'You're on the calendar. It's May 23, and here's what you're going to talk about.' I was so ter-rified, but I'd never have started unless I was bossed into it."

Heather, the transportation engineer, didn't set out look-ing for a group of mentors. But when, in her first year of graduate school, her entire department headed to Washing-ton, DC, for their industry's annual conference, she stum-bled into one. "I decided to go to the Women's Issues in Transportation Committee meeting," she recalls. New to the field and coming from a nonengineering background, she "felt lost" and thought a group of female professionals might understand. Intending just to observe, she was quickly recruited: "By the end of the meeting, they had asked me to plan a session at the next annual meeting. I thought, *it's ridiculous!* I don't even know what's important; I don't know how to find the speakers. But I'm up for a challenge."

Over the course of the next year, she stayed in close touch with the committee, about twenty women, many of them in high-ranking positions. Her conference session was a success, and she stayed involved in the group, eventually becoming secretary. A decade after her fateful first meeting, she's now the group's chair. "They're my core group of mentors," says Heather. She'd turn to group members for technical, job-related advice and professional development questions, and they actively encouraged her to seek them out.

When Heather was seeking her first job out of graduate school, she applied to an organization one group member worked for. "I hadn't said anything to her at first," Heather recalls, "because I didn't want to put her in an awkward position. I didn't know what was appropriate in terms of asking for her support. So someone came to her when they got my application, and she e-mailed me immediately. She said, 'I can't believe you didn't tell me! I would have been happy to go to bat for you, and I did. *But don't ever do that again.*'" When you've got mentors, Heather quickly learned, they want you to tap them.

Finally, the structure of a group (whether it's a networking group like Alisa's or a professional organization like Heather's) can be helpful. But it's not always necessary to get the help you want. My girlfriend has a suave and sophisticated friend who used to manage an art gallery, but whose passion wasn't on the business side: she wanted to paint. So, leveraging the connections she'd made, she reached out to her friends (some of New York's most acclaimed artists) for free painting lessons and studio visits. Even though they weren't an organized group, she was able to elicit knowledge from each of them and draw on their unique expertise. It was a top-notch education, and the artists, whom she'd befriended years before, were glad to help, especially since she was able to give back a steady stream of business advice and art world intelligence. The private tutorials helped her make rapid progress, and today she has an international art career and is represented by a gallery in the Netherlands.

Try This

- Make a list of a half-dozen people in your life you admire—and identify why. (Mary is great at closing sales, Ted knows how to navigate office politics better than anyone, Dinesh has figured out how to build relationships with the media, and so on.)

- For each, decide if you'll pursue an "organic" or "strategic" mentorship approach. If you work with them or see them regularly, you may be able to naturally deepen the relationship by asking for targeted advice or feedback. If you don't see them often, you may want to reach out with a specific request: "I really respect your opinion. Would you be willing to meet a few times a year and give me advice?"

- Think about what you can give back. Mentorship shouldn't be a one-way street. In addition to your gratitude, how can you help them? Can you boost them on social media by commenting on their blogs or retweeting their posts regularly? If their firms are looking for good job candidates, can you steer promising prospects their way? Can you keep them apprised about industry trends that may be less visible to someone higher up the ladder? Focus on what their needs are and work hard to find a way to meet them.

Step 5: Learn What Your Mentor Can Teach You

"Definitely the first month working for him, I never thought he'd be my mentor because he was such a pain in the neck." That's how Johnna Marcus, a young professional now training to be a speech therapist, recalls meeting Matt, who was the general manager at the large bookstore chain where she worked after graduating into the Great Recession. "He was a complete 180 from any manager I've ever had," she says. "He was very particular, very organized, precise, meticulous about things—he was difficult to get accustomed to. You either had to adapt or you were going to leave because you were never going to be at peace there. It was a shock to me."

She was a hard worker and had gotten along well with previous bosses, but reporting to Matt was a challenge: "I really went through times when I thought I couldn't do it." But she needed a job, and there were few alternatives; it had taken her months to land this position. So she slowly began to adapt to Matt's hard-core style. It wasn't easy, and sometimes she wasn't even sure where to begin. She'd have a three-page list of "to-dos" that seemed insurmountable.

But Matt was willing to help. "I have a hard time organizing things into concise points," says Johnna, "but that's what he taught me—'Let's bring it down to three basic ideas, three fundamental things you need to get done by this time,' and that made it easier to comprehend. He knew, too; he knew when I was getting nervous, and my mind would be going on all the things I needed to do, and he'd pick up on that and say, 'Let's take a deep breath and see what we're going to do first.'"

His focus on clarity and organization made an impact on Johnna. "It's about organizing everything so that when someone comes up to you and asks you where a sheet is from six months ago, you don't hesitate. You know where it is," she says. She also learned from his ability to adapt to what his employees really needed. "He didn't want anyone to come into his office and talk about things not related to efficiency," she recalls. "But I was in his office one time when I said, 'I'm telling you now I'm really overwhelmed.' He knew the way he needed to be at that point, he adapted, and we talked it out. He wasn't going to be [emotionally sensitive] 90 percent of the time, but the 10 percent when he needed to be, he was."

In the management jobs Johnna has held since meeting Matt, his influence is still there. "It really did sink in," she says. "I realize after all that time how much of an effect it had; his philosophies merge into yours."

Step 6: Develop Your Own Curriculum

When Roxy, the teacher-turned-fund-raiser, returned to her Women in Development group, she was astonished: "I was so excited about my mentor and I was stunned to realize I was in a minority. At least within my hearing range, everyone else was grumbling that it was terrible. No one had a good thing to say about it. I realized then that the relationship requires a lot of effort from the mentee. It's all about what you make it, ways to take hold and maximize it."

So how did she get the most out of her mentorship experience with Sally? First, she ensured their contact was frequent, with scheduled monthly breakfast meetings. (If you wait too long before contacting your mentor, the relationship may cool.) Second, and most importantly, Roxy prepared for her meetings assiduously: "I invented my own syllabus, and she was terrific at delivering these extemporaneous lectures. I'd say, 'Tell me about this, tell me about that.' The other thing I did was ask her to critique my work frequently. I'd bring her something, my plan for capital campaign materials or a draft annual fund-raising letter. I'd say, 'Are you willing to critique this? Go at it.'"

Joel would also turn to Steve with specific questions: "A lot of it was how to deal with critics, how to deal with people who'd challenge you personally, and how to communicate with an audience," he recalls. "I would come to him and say, 'Steve, I'm struggling on how to get my message across here,' and he'd help me navigate. He'd ask me questions like, 'What do you think they want? What do you have in common? What do they want to hear? How can you connect to them without giving up your position?' It was amazing advice about how to communicate with people."

Step 7: Make It Worthwhile for Your Mentor

Why do people mentor? If done right, the relationships can be tremendously rewarding. "It's some of the most enjoyable and important work I do; it's career-affirming for me," says David, the emergency department head. "I get the pleasure of watching people come in and learn to be terrific doctors and develop goals and dreams, and then actualize them. It's wonderful to watch. In a way it's like raising children, because some go on to be leaders for a whole other generation of leaders or medical students, so you can feel your efforts bearing fruit generations down."

That was certainly the case for Ben and me. When I met Ben, he was a nineteen-year-old college student who volunteered for the summer on the presidential campaign where I was working, and I snagged him for the press office. He was smart and willing to take on hard tasks like early morning "clip duty," scouring the news for relevant items to circulate to senior campaign staffers, and a willingness to drive endlessly to remote parts of New Hampshire to work events. Part of a mentor relationship (let's be honest) is about egotism, and I saw a lot of myself in Ben, from an obsession with *The New Yorker* to a concern for animal welfare. I also saw some of my flaws, such as a propensity toward too-emphatic opinions, and wanted to shield him from their consequences until he had more time to master the nuances of where and how to express them.

After the summer, he planned to leave the campaign, but I devised a scheme for a new position and lobbied the state director— quite hard—to hire Ben and give him a small salary. He became our "tracker," following our opponents and recording their every remark in order to play them back and search for mistakes. (Trackers became quite famous in 2006 when former Virginia Senator George Allen, then considered a top-rung presidential contender, insulted a tracker with what appeared to be a racial epithet, thereby destroying his chances.)

I considered it my mission to keep Ben out of harm's way, warning him sternly against underage drinking and keeping him out of the line of fire from my prickly boss. After the campaign ended, he leveraged his campaign experience into a series of public relations and marketing internships and, after graduation, an analyst job tracking congressional activity. After a couple years glued to C-SPAN, however, he decided the Beltway life wasn't for him and he was accepted to a prestigious teacher-training program. My professional utility to him is now limited, because he's teaching middle school special education, and I'm perhaps the last person you want to consult when it comes to the antics of preteenagers. But even though our mentorship has ended, I feel lucky to be his friend.

This transition to a peer-level relationship can be one of the best parts of mentorship. David recounts with delight the frequent trips he makes to hospitals across the country, doing Grand Rounds with his former students and collaborating on research. Joel, after honing his political and public relations skills by working for others for a decade, partnered professionally with Steve several years ago and eventually purchased his firm.

Step 8: Give Back

First, it starts with a simple thank you. "People underestimate the importance of that," says Roxy. "It's probably because they're humble—*what are my words to someone else?* But when I'm on the other end, mentoring someone, I wonder sometimes if they're getting anything out of it. I don't *need* to hear a thank you, but it sure feels nice. So when people mentor me, I try to give specific verbal acknowledgment, letting them know how what they said made a difference in what I was doing. Occasionally I'd give them a book or a journal, but largely it's just saying thanks."

Second, share your perspective. Michael Melcher, who befriended Dick, the power lawyer, realized he also had something to give in the relationship: "It's something to remember when dealing with older people," he says. "They like to share advice, but they're also very interested in what younger people are doing and how they view the world."

Finally, stay in touch and help where you can. Johnna wrote a recommendation for Matt on LinkedIn, a useful gesture because, like Johnna, he lost his job when their bookstore chain folded. Over time, you may be able to steer useful contacts or leads toward your mentor, and he or she will be grateful for your loyalty.

REMEMBER:

✓ Think about the skills you'd like to develop and the person you'd like to become. Who in your life embodies that? Would she be open to advising you?

✓ Look for a mentor who's focused on helping you achieve your goals, not pushing his own agenda. And be sure he's willing to make time for you. You don't want a mentor who makes you feel as if you're imposing on his time.

✓ Recognize that you may not end up with a single mentor who imparts all the necessary wisdom to you. Instead, you may need to think broadly about a group of people you can tap for different kinds of advice.

✓ Sometimes a great mentor may come in an unusual package—a younger colleague, a querulous boss. Keep an open mind and learn what she has to teach you.

✓ You have to take an active role in shaping your mentorship experience. Don't expect wisdom to simply be delivered from on high; you have to think about what you want to learn and ask good questions.

✓ Be thankful and make yourself useful. Not sure what you can give back to your mentor? Think harder. It could be assistance on a project, advising her kids about colleges, boosting his profile on social media, or helping out with grunt work—whatever would help the most.

CHAPTER 7

Leverage Your Points of Difference

Thanks to your detailed investigation, your burnished skills, and the advice of your mentors, you're beginning to develop a good sense of how you can move forward successfully into your new position or field. But your work isn't done. You've conquered the substance: identifying where you want to go and cultivating the chops necessary to get there. But that won't do you much good if the rest of the world can't see it. Now it's time to focus on rebranding yourself publicly so others recognize the new you and what you bring to the table. The first step is to understand what's unique about you, so you can convey that memorably to others.

In political campaigns (in addition to my corporate work, I've advised on presidential, gubernatorial, and US Senate bids), one of the first things you realize is that voters aren't going to take the time to evaluate all the ways you're exactly like your opponent: they're busy people and, quite rationally, they just want to know what the difference is. Some people would call this "dumbing down," but messaging specialists believe it's a positive process, because it forces (often long-winded) candidates to focus. Boiling things down and explaining why you're a compelling alternative is a powerful way to realize what's most important about you. In this chapter, you'll learn strategies for identifying and leveraging your points of difference, including:

- Building on your transferable skills

- Understanding what you have and they don't

- Using the power of your identity

- Starting with the basics: your appearance as a brand

- The perils of "fixing" your brand

Building on Your Transferable Skills

One of the key questions to ask yourself as you plot your reinvention is "What skills or experiences do I have that can be translated into my new role?" That was certainly the question Craig Della Penna faced when he learned his dream job was being eliminated. A longtime train enthusiast, Craig had been hooked on rail trails—railroad lines converted into bike paths—in the early 1990s and eventually wrote four books on the subject. When he was offered a job as a full-time rail trail advocate, it was a "pinch-me job," he recalls.

"It was more than walking the halls at the State House," he says. "It was getting to the ground level and teaching locals to move these projects ahead, to stop the antis . . . You have to travel to all these places; I was doing 900 miles a week. I'd think nothing of driving 150 miles for a public meeting to be there at 7 p.m." But when his organization announced it would be closing Craig's regional field office, he had to find another plan—fast. But if your unique skill is that you're an expert in New England rail trails, who would possibly hire you?

That's when Craig realized his special knowledge could actually serve him in many fields. Fulfilling a long-standing dream, he and his wife bought a small bed-and-breakfast in the quaint town of Northampton, Massachusetts, literally just feet from a rail trail. Marketing it as the "Sugar Maple Trailside Inn," he caters to like-minded visitors, loaning out cruiser bikes to guests and showcasing "one of the region's largest collections of antique railroad maps, documents, and books on the history of railroads in the Northeast."

As his clientele grew, Craig noticed something important. "There were a lot of guests looking to relocate here," he says. "They'd stay here and then go off with a realtor and look at purchasing a house. I thought if I became the realtor, they wouldn't leave and I'd have a more complete marketing circle—the B&B would lead to me real estate clients."

His suspicions were correct. Real estate license in hand, Craig went to work for a local firm and had a ready client base from the get-go: "I have five or six transactions per year from people who start off as B&B guests, and that allowed me to be an easy, laid-back realtor rather than a driven, shark-edged realtor." It also meant he had time to pursue the advocacy that was still his passion. "I was able to do more rail trail advocacy work after I left [the nonprofit job] than when I was working for them," he says.

He initially focused his real estate practice on selling homes near rail trails, so he could share his love of biking, leverage his extensive knowledge, and implant more advocates in local communities, an important consideration because some residents still resisted the idea of rail trails and considered them disruptive or crime-ridden. "Several antis told me they'd never be able to sell their house [near a rail trail], and I became a realtor specializing in that to tweak them," he says, laughing.

In 2010, Craig opened his own real estate office in Northampton, a franchise of a firm based in Boulder, Colorado, called Pedal to Properties, which does real estate showings by bike. "We'll tour the house, see if it's safe for kids to bike to school, check out the sights and sounds of the neighborhood," he says. Biking and rail trails are a critical part of the brand: at his request, the city removed a parking space in front of his office and he installed a fourteen-bike corral. He gives out loaner bikes to clients and to guests at local hotels, and he offers weekly bike tours showing off the local rail trail network. "They'll never put on my gravestone that I sold houses," Craig says. "I'm like the Johnny Appleseed of rail trail conversion."

From Legal Scholar to Wine Expert

Craig turned his unique knowledge about rail trails into a new career as a B&B proprietor and realtor. Lisa Granik, on the other hand, initially feared she'd have to throw away her hard-fought legal training as she considered a new direction. An aspiring law professor, she'd done all the right things— Fulbright research in the former Soviet Union, a doctorate from Yale Law School, and a hefty dissertation tracking the comparative history of sexual harassment litigation in Russia and the United States. But as she got closer to her goal, there were ominous signs. "I had several friends who were legal academics, and all of them were clearly unhappy," she recalls. "I thought, is this my future?"

She began diving into an amateur interest of hers—wine—and taking classes. And soon, she made a surprising discovery: her training as a legal scholar was the *perfect* background to launch a new career in the wine industry. First, like most academics, she'd had language training in order to be able to research primary sources. Fluent in Russian, Spanish, and French, with a little Italian thrown in, Lisa found herself uniquely positioned to communicate directly with winegrowers, many of whom are farmers who don't speak English. Second, she realized her ability to evaluate the taste of wine was shaped by her legal education. "Wine analysis is deductive," she says, "and that's a skill set one develops as a lawyer. It's the ability to break a wine down with deductive reasoning."

Third, her training in oral arguments meant she had an edge in communicating about wine: "The ability to take a complex problem and explain it to someone who's not an expert, that's a very useful skill that many people don't have." Finally, in a somewhat comic turn of events, she was even able to leverage her experience writing a dissertation. It turns out that to become a Master of Wine, a rigorous industry designation, you have to study for years, take a battery of tests, and, yes, write a dissertation about wine. Using the research skills she'd picked up on the first go-round, she was able to polish off her second one more quickly. Today, Lisa is actually the North American dissertation coordinator for the Institute of Masters of Wine.

On the surface, legal academia and the wine business have little in common. But as Lisa's story shows, sometimes the most salient job requirements are hidden below the surface and are eminently transferable.

Understand What You Have—That They Don't

Another important question you can ask is what skills or abilities you possess that are in short supply in your new field. Susan Leeds was a Wharton MBA who had worked for more than fifteen years as an investment banker: "credit products, fixed-income security, municipal bonds," she'd done it all. After taking several years off with her kids, she was looking for a new direction. "I didn't want to go back and do what I did before," she says. "If I'm going to go back to work and not be with my kids, I'm going to do something I care about—something that motivates me and feels like I'm making a difference."

As a new mother, she had developed an interest in environmental issues: "I started thinking about what's happening in the world, and what kind of a world our children are going to grow up in." Casually tooling around on the website of an environmental advocacy group, she stumbled onto a job listing: astonishingly, they were looking for someone with an investment banking background. Soon, Susan was on the job with a two-year policy fellowship.

It was an immediate culture shock. She'd never worked at a nonprofit, never done policy research, and had taken a massive pay cut. "I was a terrible fish out of water at that place," she recalls. "There were four hundred employees and only two MBAs—one in accounting and the other was me." She wasn't always received positively: "I was a suspect person. I'm in a world of hard-core environmental advocates and I was from the business world; there were plenty of people in the environmental advocacy field who view people like me as the enemy. I was learning to speak a different language and getting frustrated because people didn't understand what I was saying or didn't care about my opinion."

Determined to succeed at her fellowship, she muscled through: "I focused on the positive aspects as much as I could, that this role was giving me the opportunity to meet and network with a huge number of people, some of them senior level, that I otherwise would have never had access to. And I also focused on the fact that I cared about the work."

But amid the lawyers, policy wonks, and scientists, she realized she had a special skill: "They wanted someone who could talk to people on Wall Street, and I could do that." She also saw important connections to her old job. "One of the big opportunities was making buildings more energy efficient," she says. "You invest in them and all of a sudden, it looks a lot like real estate finance and asset finance, and that's what I know how to do. Most of the policy work that looked at how to increase investment in energy efficiency was being done by traditionalists, and they weren't looking at it as investments. It was about forcing people to do it, rather than a market-based perspective. *You can make an investment associated with a positive return*—that became my mantra, that you have to look at things differently."

She began to develop a reputation as an innovative thinker in the field. Before her fellowship was up, she had become a coveted speaker at major conferences and multiple firms had headhunted her. Today, she runs a public-private partnership dedicated to spurring energy efficiency investments. "It's a huge learning experience. I knew a lot about financial markets, but it's also now about government, policy, energy, utilities, regulation, and even the real estate industry," she says. "People look to me for policy leadership in this field, and that's a different thing than I would have done in a million years on Wall Street."

Leverage Your Outsider Status

Susan's finance skills, while top-notch, weren't unusual on Wall Street. But she made herself valuable because in the environmental advocacy world, very few people knew what she did. Her skills became a precious commodity that distinguished her and helped her rise quickly. In a similar fashion, Jason Shaplen leveraged his unique position as a newcomer in various fields. Most professions judge you on your experience—in that profession. But Jason knew he could never win that game.

The real question was, how do you take an eclectic résumé (he had worked as a journalist, a management consultant, diplomatic negotiator, presidential campaign speechwriter, Asian telecom executive, and nonprofit executive) and turn it into a strength, rather than a weakness? His answer was to simultaneously allay concerns about his competence, while intriguing others with his outsider perspective.

"I've worked in so many fields, I can speak the language of almost any of them," he says. "I can talk to the hedge fund guy in his language, or I can go to the governor's office and talk in his language about moving things through the legislature. As I meet new people, in part because I can talk a little bit of their language, they start being interested in you: *He talks like a diplomat, but not a standard diplomat—maybe he can help us think about things differently.* I guess I give people confidence that I know enough about their field, yet I can bring something new and interesting to the table."

He worked hard to learn the nuances of his new professions. "It was total immersion," he says. "I ran like hell for the library." But he also embraced his outsider role, which he knew gave him the freedom to suggest new ideas and approaches. "I try to keep myself out of the minutiae, to make sure there's enough distance so I have some perspective," he says. "You have to know how to do the mechanics, but you also want to think about it in a new way. So you actually try *not* to become an expert in the field. You want to be something in between: halfway between being an expert and being a total novice. It's knowing enough to know what's going to make a difference and be helpful, but you're still able to think outside the box."

He's used that technique in his current role as executive director of a homelessness prevention agency. Even though he's now worked in the field for nearly a decade—long enough to amass a great deal of expertise—he still tries to maintain an outsider's perspective, looking for innovations from other industries. "We've created a fantastic new model for how to serve homeless children," he says, "and that's because I go look at how things are done in early childhood education programs, child guidance centers, centers helping kids in crisis, and that's typically not done in our field."

Use the Power of Your Identity

Above and beyond your skills and unique experiences, there's something else you can draw on to distinguish yourself: your core identity. Sometimes, there are contributions only you can make. That was the case for Naif Al-Mutawa, a native of

Kuwait who always wanted to be a writer. In his twenties, fired up by a news report about a local man losing his dry-cleaning job because of his religion, Naif wrote an illustrated book about the importance of diversity, which eventually won a UNESCO prize for children's literature in the service of tolerance. He won a contract for two additional books, but still considered it a side project. "My parents said it was a great hobby, but not to think about it for work," he recalls.

By 2003, with several psychology degrees under his belt ("as close as I could get to writing and characters"), Naif thought he'd put his literary days behind him. But one day, while he was riding in a cab with his sister, she encouraged him to write another children's book. He'd also earned an MBA from Columbia in the interim, and his mind immediately jumped to the cost-benefit analysis: "I said, 'It would have to be something that has the potential of Pokemon; otherwise it wouldn't make sense to write another book,'" he recalls. "It was basically my way of saying, 'Shut up.'" But the idea began to grow on him. It turned out that Pokemon, the viral children's phenomenon, wasn't allowed in some Arab countries. What if, in the aftermath of 9/11, he could create a universal story line from an Islamic perspective?

That idea turned into *The 99,* a group of superheroes with a Middle Eastern and Islamic flavor who display "wisdom, generosity, and the basic human values we all share," he says. The goal? "We're competing for the hearts and minds of the next generation, who are sometimes taught to use religion for hate." *The 99* began as a comic book series and, indeed, has become a Pokemon-like phenomenon, spinning off an animated television show that airs globally and a theme park. *The 99* has even been praised as an emblem of tolerance by President Obama. "I made sure that from the very beginning it was crafted for a global audience, knowing it could go global if there were the right circumstances," says Naif.

It might seem like a stretch for a psychologist—even one with an MBA—to create a global brand of Islamic superheroes. But his experience as an Arab living in America provided the inspiration, his business school connections helped him raise funds, and his psychology training gave him the insights he needed to create compelling story lines. "The characters all come with conflicts and problems. It's all the theories I learned in organizational psychology," he says. Naif's experience and worldwide success show the power of drawing on every part of your personal experience to create your next professional identity.

Naif is a perfect example of drawing from one's unique background and perspective. After 9/11, the world was practically crying out for a social-justice-loving Arab psychologist with an MBA to create Muslim superheroes. But you can draw powerfully from your own identity even if it's unrelated to world historical forces. That was certainly the case for Hank Phillippi Ryan, the TV reporter inspired to write by her young producer.[1]

The Story Only You Can Tell

Ryan, captivated by Agatha Christie and Arthur Conan Doyle as a girl, had always wanted to write mysteries. It took well over two decades as a TV news reporter to take the plunge. But when her first novel was released, it was a hit, winning a prestigious Agatha Award, due in large part to her likable heroine Charlotte "Charlie" McNally, an older female

TV reporter coping with the pressures of staying relevant in a youth-obsessed industry.

"The only reason these books are as textured, thoughtful, reflective, and honest as they are is that the person who is me *now* can write that," says Hank, now in her early sixties and the author of several popular novels. "Twenty years ago, I was such a different person. I wouldn't have written these things; the attitude would have been completely different. I'm writing about a woman in midlife, a TV reporter, facing the possibility the camera doesn't love her anymore. Since I *was* that twenty years ago, it was impossible for me to face that. I would have fought it, but now I embrace it."

Start with the Basics—Your Appearance as a Brand

Some might say it makes sense for you to base your brand on skills or experiences or important parts of your identity. You've worked hard to develop them through commitment and hard work (like Susan's mastery of real estate finance), or they're reflective of key values you hold (like Naif's commitment to a tolerant Islam). But what if your brand is shaped, in others' minds, by factors outside your control? What if, regardless of your preferences, others insist on noticing something extraneous? The only solution is to recognize what others are seeing and take control of your brand.

I frequently hear from executives who are concerned they may be viewed negatively because of physical characteristics or fundamental traits. It's certainly easier to break in if you fit the mold—the preppy, white, hedge fund guy;

the vaguely dorky IT genius; or the sexy blonde saleswoman. But what I've also seen is this: it's much harder to stand out. How are you different from the other preppy white guys? You'll have to work hard to make the case. But if you manage to break in and your difference is obvious, you're already attracting the attention you need to build a powerful brand. Your presumed weakness can, in fact, become your strength. That's what happened with my former employer, Robert Reich.

I worked as Reich's press secretary when he ran for Massachusetts governor. From the beginning, voters and the media were fascinated by him. He was already a national celebrity, having served as US Labor Secretary in President Clinton's administration and then writing a revealing memoir about his experiences. The public was keen to meet him and see him in action. But he knew from long experience that when he entered a room, they were in for a surprise. Everyone knew Reich was short; he'd even jokingly titled his memoir *Locked in the Cabinet*. But he wasn't "short for a guy." He was *very short*—4 feet, $10^1/_2$ inches, to be specific. And if you're trying to win someone's vote, you don't want them to feel shocked or uncomfortable, because it distracts from the message you're trying to deliver about jobs or health care or the environment.

So Bob, with his trademark humor, would raise the subject first. He'd crack jokes about his height so the audience would laugh with him, not at him. (He even published a book of essays during the campaign entitled *I'll Be Short*.) In the process, he established himself as a different kind of politician, one who doesn't take himself too seriously. He took a physical trait that could have held him back—after all, politics is rife with the adage that the "taller candidate always wins"—and instead used it to his advantage, making him uniquely memorable. "I like that short guy," voters would muse. "He's really smart." (He didn't end up winning the nomination. But then again, neither did any of the other, taller white guys. They all lost to a candidate who was even more differentiated: a woman.)

Marketing guru Seth Godin, who is completely bald, has similarly taken a noticeable physical characteristic and made it part of his brand. Two of his books feature his head—just from the eyes up—on their covers, and on his website, you're instructed to "Click on Seth's head to read his blog!"[2] If someone is going to notice your physical traits anyway, you might as well control the conversation.

Try This

- Make a list of the things about yourself that most surprise people when you tell them at cocktail parties (you were in the Peace Corps, you can speak Finnish, you're a former professional saxophonist).

- Now write down your professional skills—the things you might tout to a recruiter (you're a terrific negotiator, you have deep management expertise, you code faster than anyone). List at least two "proof points" for each—a story you can tell that demonstrates your expertise vividly.

- Mix and match your lists. As you think about your future goals, which align best? Which combinations are most interesting, surprising, or memorable? (People aren't likely to forget a Finnish-speaking, jazz-playing computer programmer.)

The Perils of "Fixing" Your Brand

Sometimes, there may be a temptation to fix what others might perceive as a physical shortcoming. But proceed with caution. It turns out that those elements may actually be a crucial part of your brand, making you memorable and likable. That's what happened with Jennifer Grey, who was a famous actress in the 1980s, starring as Ferris Bueller's sister and, most iconically, as "Baby," the sheltered young woman who falls for Patrick Swayze in *Dirty Dancing*.

In a world of Stepford-like actresses, Grey was special: she had a distinctive nose that flouted all the supposed Hollywood requirements. At first, her appearance hurt her film career. "I was too Jewish for *Flashdance*," Grey told the *New York Times* in 1987. "I didn't even make it in to see Zeffirelli for *Endless Love*. His assistant said, "'Sorry, we're looking for a beautiful girl.'"[3] But all that changed after *Dirty Dancing*, a surprise hit that she seemed destined to play. "I became recognizable, known and loved by so many people," she said. "I didn't look like a movie star. I had a Jewish nose. People loved seeing that."[4]

But, ultimately, she felt the need to change it. In the 1990s, she had a rhinoplasty that altered the way she looked so drastically that many people considered her unrecognizable. She was pretty, sure, but she didn't look like Jennifer Grey. This scenario (fairly dire for an actress whose face is her brand) became such a running joke in Hollywood, she was actually cast as a fictionalized version of herself in the short-lived TV show *It's Like, You Know...*, playing an actress with a stalled career. In 2010, more than twenty years after her *Dirty Dancing* success, her footwork paid off again: she won the coveted *Dancing with the Stars* competition on TV, raising her profile and ensuring that people would finally recognize the "new" Jennifer Grey. But still, newspapers reported, she said that getting a new nose was the worst mistake she had ever made.[5]

In a competitive marketplace, no one is interested in how you're the same as everyone else. Though it may be human to want to downplay your differences, that may actually extinguish part of what makes you successful. Embrace your differences, and you can turn them into your strengths.

REMEMBER:

- ✓ Think creatively about your skills. Being a legal scholar doesn't just mean you know the law; it means you speak multiple languages, are great at deductive reasoning, and can make articulate oral arguments. How do those abilities translate to your new professional goal?

- ✓ The branding terrain may have changed. Unique attributes from five years ago (you know how to blog!) may have become commonplace. What's distinct about you in today's marketplace?

- ✓ Ask yourself: what do you have that they don't? Turn around your opponents' arguments. If they say you can't make it in the nonprofit world because you've only worked on Wall Street, that's likely the exact reason you'll succeed; you bring value no one else does.

✓ Think about the power of your personal identity. Is there a contribution only you can make because of your unique mix of background, skills, and experience?

✓ If you're different from others in your desired field (such as a woman in venture capital), you may find it harder to break in. But you're likely to be more memorable and successful once you're in the door.

✓ If your appearance is unusual and likely to be noticed by others, don't shy away from acknowledging it, and don't rush to change it. That element may be an important part of what makes your brand memorable.

CHAPTER 8

Build Your Narrative

Now that you've identified the unique talent, skill, or perspective that sets you apart from everyone else in your space, it's time to craft a powerful story that explains it. Humans understand the world around them through stories, narratives we tell ourselves about what's happening and why. So when we come upon discordant information or stories that don't make sense, it can be perplexing and annoying. In fact, as Malcolm Gladwell famously wrote in *The Tipping Point,* kids who are confused by the action they see on television will simply turn away and disengage. For better or for worse, adults aren't much different.

As you seek to rebrand yourself, you're going to have to come up with a convincing narrative to explain your transformation, whether it's a small one (I was an engineer, and now I want to develop my management and supervisory skills), or something huge (I used to run a yoga studio, but now I've decided to work on Wall Street). I use the word *convincing* deliberately: of course, your choices are valid, regardless of what others think. But, like the proverbial tree falling in the forest, your rebranding isn't going to do you much good if other people don't get it or choose to ignore it.

Consequently, you need to take a step back and construct a story that others can understand and appreciate. No one condones murder, but they can at least understand if a man is avenging his wife's killer (and, of course, that's the plot of many movies). People may not think it's wise for you to abandon your 401(k) and job security, but they can respect it if you're following a long-standing dream. And they might not even think you're qualified to become a management consultant if you've previously been a poet, but your story can and should convince them it's the right move. So how do you do it? In this chapter, you'll learn how to:

- Make the connections between your past and present obvious to others

- Find the hidden, underlying themes that connect your professional experiences

- Explain your trajectory in terms of the value you bring to others

Plus, we'll cover:

- You can't be who you aren't

- You have to believe in yourself

- Embodying your new brand

Make the Connections Obvious

When Toby Johnson graduated from West Point, her first job out of college was the furthest thing possible from entry-level paper pushing: she became an Apache helicopter pilot, the only woman in a class of thirty trainees. Her performance—over seven years in the army, including a tour in Iraq—won raves. She was lauded by her supervisors and was even featured in an army advertising campaign. But when she decided to leave the military to attend business school, she faced one big disadvantage compared to her classmates, many of whom entered with corporate experience: "The only big organization I'd ever worked for was the United States Army."

So how do you compete for job offers with talented peers who have clear, compelling stories to tell about their time in the corporate world? After all, flying a helicopter may not seem directly relevant to corporate success. Toby knew the lessons were transferable, but she'd have to connect the dots for potential employers. Her mission was to create a narrative that both made sense and captivated them. "I used my military experience as an advantage," she says.

She had to craft a story that made sense to skeptical hiring managers, stressing the management experience she'd gained in the military (at age twenty-four, she was in charge of eight $30 million Apache helicopters, plus the thirty people who managed them) and the rapid learning made possible by her early leadership experience. Many of her peers, trying management out for the first time, wouldn't yet have found their unique style and could make some costly mistakes in the interim.

In other words, Toby took charge of her story and ensured that what was clear to her (she's building on her management and leadership experience and taking it to a new arena) was also understandable to others (who might otherwise question what a helicopter pilot could bring to a corporation). Her strategy worked; today, she's a fast-rising executive at a multinational consumer goods company.

Find Your Hidden, Underlying Themes

As Toby's experience shows, there are often underlying themes that guide us professionally. They may not be obvious to others, who are too busy making surface-level connections. But it's essential that we take the time to spell them out, because consistency and reliability are considered fundamental virtues in the workforce. Even if we're changing careers or making a fairly dramatic leap up the corporate ladder, we can gain understanding, respect, and support if we show others we're following a clear path. That was the case for John Davidow, a public radio executive who, in his fifties, took on a new professional challenge.

Think "internet expert" and you're likely to conjure up a hoodie-clad millennial. So when John, a veteran of traditional media for three decades, was appointed to head up online operations at his station, it may have raised some eyebrows. But he embraced the change eagerly, in part because of his sense that the new online world wasn't a break with his media past but, rather, a continuation of it. "My whole career, I've been a bit of a nonconformist," he says. He began his career in TV news at the start of the satellite era and "we were in many ways defining what local television news was. There still weren't really rules of the road."

He sensed that same liminal potential in the online world. "This stuff I'm doing now—online news, engagement, storytelling—it's all reminiscent of that time when there were so many creative opportunities." Even though the tools may be different (social media instead of satellite trucks), the basics of creating a powerful news experience are the same. So John isn't a newbie digital executive with only a few years of experience. Instead, he argues he's been doing the same thing for his entire career: telling stories and being a change agent. "I've always been most effective when I'm working in places with fewer grown-ups," he says. "That way we're able to innovate and create. This is simply a new way to be engaged and challenged and entrepreneurial."

Extending Your "Product Line"

John showed how executives can gain credibility in a new field by highlighting less obvious connections to their past experience. Well known author Tim Ferriss's experience is an example of a related strategy: extending your product line.

Ferriss was a guy always looking for shortcuts. While growing up on Long Island, he was obsessed with topics like learning new languages and speed reading. How could you do it better? Faster? Weren't there best practices and loopholes you could exploit? Still in his twenties, he'd founded BrainQUICKEN, an online sports nutrition company he says brought in $40,000 per month, but was making him tired, overworked, and miserable. On a long-awaited European vacation, Ferriss writes, he had "a nervous breakdown the first morning" because of his pent-up stress, prompting him to kick-start a new, more strategic way of living. Thus was born his blockbuster *The 4-Hour Workweek: Escape 9–5, Live Anywhere, and Join the New Rich,* a paean to "life-hacking" your way to fame, fortune, and leisure.

The 4-Hour Workweek is technically a business book, and that's where Ferriss, leveraging his start-up street cred, originally gained fame. (Indeed, an early *New York Times* profile highlights the extreme—and counterintuitive—devotion he inspired among the Silicon Valley elite, given his recommendation to sharply limit e-mail consumption and embark upon a "low-information diet."[1]) The book puts forward productivity tips that certainly could juice up your professional life: hiring virtual assistants from India, creating a profitable online business, convincing your boss to let you work from home, managing time, and setting goals, to name just a few.

But it's clear Ferriss's interests and inspirations are wide-ranging. He touts international travel and the benefits of "geoarbitrage"—that is, making money in American dollars and spending it in cheaper locales. He encourages readers not to wait until they're sixty-five to fulfill their travel fantasies, but instead to take "mini-retirements" and embrace a mobile lifestyle in which they can work from anywhere. He touts the virtues of language study (he speaks five, and on his blog, shares techniques for hacking the process to learn more quickly) and learning sports or mastering other forms of local culture (two of his favorites are Argentine tango and Japanese horseback archery). It's a vision that's hard to resist. So once you've cultivated a passionate fan base and a sterling brand as a business author (*Fast Company* named him one of the "Most Innovative Business People of 2007"), what do you do?

If you're Tim Ferriss, you write a diet and exercise book. Say what?

Bridging Your Brand Gap

On the surface, Ferriss's choice of sequel might seem bizarre. After all, he's not a doctor, a nutrition coach, or a famous athlete (though he does recount an incident in *The 4-Hour Workweek* in which he wins the gold medal at the 1999 Chinese Kickboxing National Championships by exploiting a technicality and pushing his opponent off an elevated platform). But his newer work—*The 4-Hour Body: An Uncommon Guide to Rapid Fat-Loss, Incredible Sex, and Becoming Superhuman*—can actually be viewed as a savvy next step for someone who refuses to be boxed in.

"I don't want to put out 'The $3^1/_2$ Hour Workweek' or 'The 3-Hour Workweek.' It would be boring for me to produce and it would be boring, I think, for many people to consume," Ferriss told the *Signal vs. Noise* blog, run by the trendy software firm 37signals.[2] Ferriss was hungry for a new challenge and—just as he advised his readers to avoid the stagnation of jobs they didn't enjoy—strove to avoid a long-term career recycling the same bromides.

"A big part of it [*The 4-Hour Body*] was diversifying my identity," he said. "I didn't want to paint myself into a corner where I felt obligated to maintain a certain level of 'success.' Even if *The 4-Hour Body* were to do far worse than *The 4-Hour Workweek*, I felt this was a necessary step for my own personal preservation. I also wanted to diversify the public perception of my expertise. I want people, hopefully, to read my material because of the way I deconstruct problems, not because of the specific subject matter. I would rather be in the same vein as Malcolm Gladwell or George Plimpton than someone who's known for just being an expert in one subject matter." Ferriss used three winning strategies in extending his brand, so that the transition was understandable and palatable to readers.

First, he built on the already-recognizable "4-Hour" brand, forcing readers to see a commonality between his books, despite their different subject matter. Second, he rose above the narrow confines of being a business author and created his own category. It's a huge leap from "business" to "health." But viewed another way, it's just a logical continuation of Ferriss's expertise in "lifestyle design," a term he invented to encompass creating the best lifestyle with the least amount of time, effort, and money (and own a new search engine category, since topics like "productivity" were already saturated). And third, Ferriss branched out strategically. In August 2011, he signed a much-vaunted deal with Amazon's new publishing arm for his third book, *The 4-Hour Chef.* Going directly from the business aisle to writing a cookbook would be a radical departure, but Ferriss prepared his readers (and built a ready audience of buyers) with the transitional *4-Hour Body,* bridging the gap by applying business-style productivity tips to fitness.

The wider world would have been happy to label Ferriss a business author and wonder why he'd ever want to write health and fitness books. But Ferriss, in claiming a new identity and category for himself, was able to argue that he wasn't making a radical leap, just building on a direction he'd already started.

Explain the Value You Bring

The last crucial piece in telling your story is explaining that your change isn't simply a sign of narcissism. Everyone has passions and things they'd love to do. It's nice to be fulfilled, but it's also nice to be an adult and pay your mortgage. So how can you get people to care? To respect your decision? To take you seriously? *You have to explain it's not about you; it's about the value you bring.*

That was the challenge facing Libby Wagner, a Seattle-based poet who made a transition into management consulting. A tenured community college professor who taught poetry, women's studies, and creative writing, she literally could have kept her job forever. But when her sister died of breast cancer, she realized she needed a change.

During her time in academia, she'd been responsible for developing a statewide program for instructor development. The state department of corrections took notice and recruited her to oversee employee development and training. "Everyone was like, 'What? Giving up your tenured job and selling your house?'" Soon, she also questioned her decision; within a few months, she realized it wasn't a fit. "The only reason I succeeded in academia was the autonomy; there was no time clock, and I could set my schedule," she recalls. "But I wouldn't have described myself as an entrepreneur; I didn't have that language. On a college campus, MBAs don't hang out with poets; we don't think we have anything in common."

But at the department of corrections, she threw herself into the world of MBAs. When her boss warned Libby that her job was in jeopardy due to budget cuts, "I took advantage of every possible professional development opportunity

I could get my hands on while I was still working. I made a commitment to learn everything I could about this world I was entering into, that was very different than academia." She joined professional groups and drilled into the minutiae of the job. "It was like management boot camp," she says. "There was every possible weird employee issue; it was like a petri dish."

Eventually, she decided to launch her own consulting business. She'd picked up enough chops and management lingo during her time at the department of corrections to be convincing as a consultant, but she was still ashamed to open up about her past life. "I didn't want anyone to know I was a poet," she says. "I had a lot of tapes going in my head. The economists I had worked with had really talked down to me, and people in business certainly weren't interested in what I did. I was so afraid. In the very beginning, I thought I should try to go to Harvard and get an MBA." But she held off and decided to try without it.

Soon, she realized that her clients weren't asking about her credentials: "When they see that what I do actually works, then nobody cares. Nobody has ever asked me if I have an MBA, ever." In fact, she says, "I think my not having an MBA gives me an advantage; I can ask all the 'new girl' questions and it makes them step out of their paradigm for a little while to see if what they're doing is working for them."

And it turns out the very skills she honed as a poet were the ones most relevant in her consulting. "The way I see the world is very language-driven," she says. "I'm going to be listening for nuances and connections and patterns. That's the way I look at the world and I take that to any interaction with the client, so I've learned to ask really good questions."

Today, Libby has consulted for *Fortune* 500 clients including Boeing and Nike, and she's christened her monthly e-newsletter *The Boardroom Poet*. The secret to embracing her own narrative from poet to consultant was embracing the value she could bring to her clients. As she wrote in a recent essay, "my clients want results. They want to know that the money, time and effort they are going to invest will give them what they want: higher profits, more engaged workplaces, less stress, success in their endeavors. I can do this, exactly as I am . . . When I show up as a poet, entrepreneur, and ordinary smart person, I can then help others be who they need to be, too."[3]

Your Road-to-Damascus Moment

Sometimes, your narrative reveals a linear transition (Toby going from leading soldiers to leading executives, or Libby using the power of language, first in poetry and then in management consulting). Other times, it just doesn't. Your transition may be harsh, abrupt, and shocking, and the only explanation you can offer is the truth: something powerful changed in you.

"She must have been in her early twenties," recalls Phyllis Stein, the career counselor. Her client wanted to break into the music industry, but her reasons were poorly developed; she mostly seemed drawn to its glamor. "We had about three sessions, and then I didn't hear from her. I didn't know what happened until she came back six months later. She'd been in a major automobile accident, and she wanted to pick up with the work we'd done."

But, after spending months in the hospital and enduring painful surgeries, her priorities had changed completely, and the music industry no longer interested her. Says Stein, "She went from frivolous to very, very serious about taking science classes in order to do the work she wanted to do in medicine. It was dramatic, the growth and maturity."

The most famous sudden transformation dates to the story of Saul in the Christian Bible, who was heading from Jerusalem on the road to Damascus to arrest supporters of Jesus. While in transit, he is struck down by a light from heaven and suddenly comes to believe that Jesus is the Son of God. He feels compelled to publicly proclaim his new belief and thereby becomes St. Paul, one of the most famous evangelists in church history. Most "rebranding revelations"

Try This

- Write down your explanation—no more than two sentences—about why you're making a transition. Stay away from self-indulgent story lines; highlight how you want to apply your skills to new domains or learn new things.

- What's the value you bring? Write down one or two sentences identifying the unique knowledge or skills you have that others in your new domain might not.

- Find your common thread. You're not rejecting one identity in favor of another; you're transitioning across an isthmus linking the old and new brands. How can you articulate that commonality?

- Practice telling your story to close friends. Does it sound plausible? Responsible? Strategic? You want honest feedback; your goal is something that will sound compelling and make sense even to people you're meeting for the first time.

aren't divine, of course, but they often involve a dramatic humbling and the lessons learned from it.

No one seeks out an accident, or an addiction, or (in the case of fallen-then-redeemed lifestyle guru Martha Stewart) a stint in prison. But in some cases, those dramatic and painful events can lead to true growth and a meaningful change in how you, and others, see yourself.

The First Caveat: You Can't Be Who You Aren't

With all this talk about rebranding yourself and crafting a narrative to explain your transition, there might be a tempta tion to go all out. If you're in rebranding mode, why not become the person you've always wanted to be? Why not become the *perfect person?* I'm a fan of self-improvement; that's why I wrote this book. But it's important to caution that there are limits to reinvention. You can't simply concoct a new personality, and in our society, there's nothing worse than a phony. Your friends and colleagues will notice (and be appalled), and in our increasingly connected world, it's safe to say that others will hear about it, as well.

All that seems obvious, but the message still hasn't reached some powerful executives (who imagine they can simply decree a new identity) or high-level politicians (who turn their personas over to smooth-talking Svengali consultants). One of these execs is Alex Bogusky, the wunderkind impresario behind the advertising agency Crispin Porter + Bogusky. His firm created innovative campaigns for brands like Virgin Atlantic, Burger King, and Volkswagen, and was named *Advertising Age*'s "Agency of the Decade." But in early 2010, Bogusky decided to leave it all behind. Danielle Sacks, a *Fast*

Company writer, had interviewed Bogusky two years earlier in a cover story, declaring him "the Steve Jobs of the Ad World." But this time, she said, "It quickly became clear that he was not the same man I had written about . . . Back then, he had been as clever, brash, and iconoclastic as the campaigns that earned him a reputation as the most dangerous weapon in advertising . . . Yet the Bogusky sitting before me in Manhattan sounded more like some of the activists I'd interviewed in this era of financial and environmental crises. Instead of talking brands, Bogusky riffed on the inequities of Wall Street, the flaws of corporate structure, and the need for social and environmental transparency. He was a man released, trying on the clothes of a new and as yet undefined life."[4]

Bogusky, a denizen of eco-conscious Boulder, Colorado, has embraced a new life as an investor in green start-ups and the proprietor of the FearLess Cottage, a gathering place for people Bogusky would like to hang with (each entry card reads, "The recipients of this card have demonstrated that they are capable of pushing aside fear in pursuit of doing the right thing"). He recounted to *Fast Company* his realization that his advertising work conflicted with his emerging consciousness about the dangers of fast food and sodas: "You compromise your voice slowly over time," he said, "and then you have a moment where you're like, 'Wow, that really isn't what I think' . . . I heard my mouth disconnected from my soul."

It sounds like a classic midlife crisis story—a successful multimillionaire taking laudable steps to configure his life to better reflect his values. Bogusky, slightly teary, conceded as much to *Fast Company*: "I fear a moment when my children are older, and they look at me and say, 'What did you do? The world is like a spiraling cesspool. You were an adult, you needed to do something. I was just a kid. What did you do?' I want to be able to say, I did this, this, and this. And did my best."

But halfway through a fairly typical profile of a changed man, tinged with newfound Zen consciousness, we get something radically different. "I'm back in New York," writes Sacks, "doing follow-up interviews by phone, and a former Crispin senior creative has been ranting for more than two hours about the 'phony life wrecker' he used to work for. As I continue calling around, it becomes apparent that all those hours of candid, 'fearless' reckoning I shared with Bogusky may not have been quite as fearless or as candid as I thought."

It doesn't seem to be one or two disgruntled employees that have it in for Bogusky. Sacks quotes a variety of former colleagues (all unnamed, claiming a fear of retribution) who decry him in terms such as "megalomaniac, sociopath, [and] narcissist" and compare him to Fidel Castro, Caligula, and Hannibal Lecter. They describe an abusive boss who manipulated staff, created a sweatshop environment, and didn't hesitate to humiliate people in public.

If that were anything close to the truth, it wouldn't be a bad idea for Bogusky to revamp his brand and consider some new ways of doing business. But unlike lifestyle maven Martha Stewart's road-to-Damascus experience, in which she appeared to genuinely learn from her fall from grace, Bogusky is portrayed as clueless about his own culpability and indifferent to the impact he had on others. "Toward the end of our talk," Sacks writes, "I press to see if he feels any remorse. 'Do I feel bad about how I've treated some of my employees in the past?' he responds, taking an uncharacteristically long pause. 'I want to say yes, but I'm not feeling that.'"

How Al Gore Lost—Then Found—His Branding Mojo

Politicians have a notoriously hard time reinventing their brands. The public and the press just don't buy it, but that doesn't stop campaigns from trying. (Case in point: the uproar sparked by an aide to Mitt Romney, who glibly declared to CNN that his candidate's positions could be recalibrated just like an Etch-a-Sketch.)

In 2000, Al Gore was also a conflicted man. He'd built up a solid reputation: eight years as a competent vice president, dutifully spearheading initiatives on things like improving government efficiency. But his predecessor, Bill Clinton, loomed large. Gore was stiff and patrician where Clinton was loose and accessible. And though at the time Gore himself had a reputation for marital rectitude, he still feared being tarred with the tumult of Clinton's Monica Lewinsky scandal and subsequent investigation. So how do you harness the best elements of Bill Clinton's brand without taking on the worst? Gore made the obvious choice and turned to Bob Shrum.

Shrum was a storied Democratic consultant, who had risen to fame as a speechwriter (crafting Ted Kennedy's immortal "The Dream Shall Never Die" speech) and eventually became an overall consigliere and mastermind, raking in handsome fees and spurring insecure candidates to enter into the "Shrum Primary," in which they would beg, plead, and outbid each other in order to win Shrum for their team. Of course, there was also an underbelly—the "Shrum Curse." Shrum was not part of Bill Clinton's team and couldn't claim credit for his victory. Instead, his track record, at least at the presidential level, was dismal. (Now retired, his grand total was eight losing presidential campaigns.) But he had nonetheless become a powerhouse, an éminence grise, and a favorite of the establishment.

Part of the knock on Shrum was that he forced his candidates into a mold, prompting them to sound alike and mouth words that just didn't sound right for them. It's easy to look back now, especially after watching the carnage of the John Kerry presidential campaign, which Shrum also shepherded. But in the heat of battle during the 2000 election, Al Gore—so frustrated by the weak image his eight years of second-bananahood had wrought that he turned to feminist author Naomi Wolf for sartorial advice—made what he thought was a sound choice. He allowed Shrum to reshape him into a fire-breathing crusader for "working families," dramatically speechifying about "The People vs. the Powerful."

"The battle lines are drawn," Shrum told the *New York Times* that summer. "Al Gore comes out of the convention much more clearly defined to people. There's a choice on a thematic dimension: Who's going to stand up and fight for middle-class families on prescription drugs, a patients' bill of rights and education?"[5]

The problem was, no one bought it. Gore, known to Americans for well over a decade as a friendly-but-bland policy wonk obsessed with the environment, was simply not believable as a populist cowboy, ready to 'rassle with

George W. Bush. There are limits to how far your brand can stretch. Tim Ferriss can make a good case that business productivity and "hacking your body" are linked. And Gore surely could have tweaked his image to bolster his alpha-male credentials in less obvious ways. But when you go too far, you risk looking like a fake. At that point, you've lost all credibility.

Despite Gore's heartbreak in Florida and the loss of the presidency, there is a happy ending to his brand reinvention. Returning to his passion of environmental advocacy and "re-rebranding" himself as the dedicated policy wonk he always was, he regained his mojo and became the subject of an Oscar-winning film and recipient of the Nobel Peace Prize. Patience—and being honest with yourself about your real interests, personality, and brand—can pay inspiring dividends.

The Second Caveat: You Have to Believe in Yourself

Self-doubt is extremely common, even among the people you'd least expect. Years ago, when the start-up where Alisa Cohn had been working announced that all employees had to relocate to San Francisco—or else—she got the push she needed to start her own executive coaching business. But, at only twenty-seven, Cohn quickly felt the pressure: people expected their advice to come from sage graybeards, not recent grads. "The first few times people asked what I did," she recalls, "I said, 'I'm a coach?' in that up-talk way we do when we're not so sure—asking permission, 'Is it OK to be a coach?'" She found solace commiserating with a doctor friend who faced the same situation. As her friend advised her, "there's a distinction between being a med student and as soon as you graduate, saying 'I'm a doctor.' But you start saying that and it's an identity shift for you; at first you don't believe it. But people begin to treat you like a doctor."

So Cohn took the advice. "I'd begin to say to people, a little less diffidently, 'I'm an executive coach.' And they'd ask me more about it, so I had to learn to talk about my profession. If they were really interested, they began to treat me, as young as I was, like a coach, and they'd talk about their situation. So I began to have more confidence in myself as a coach." She was so uncomfortable with promoting her new business, it took her nearly two years before she sent out a mass e-mail to her friends and contacts, letting them know about her new business ("I had this idea that people would say, 'Can't she settle down?'"). But more than a decade later, Cohn now has a thriving practice coaching high-level *Fortune* 500 executives.

As Cohn's example shows, self-doubt has almost no relation to your skills or talents; she was perfectly capable of coaching executives effectively when she started her business. But the hardest part of making a transition can be bridging the gap between how others used to perceive you (and how you used to perceive yourself) and how you'd like to be seen moving forward. The answer? Fake it till you make it. That doesn't imply deception or disingenuousness. Instead, it recognizes that there's a time lag between fully inhabiting the "old you" and the "new you." Until you really get comfortable with the new identity, the best course is to pretend that you're already there.

In other words, contrary to most people's fears, people are not looking to nitpick your identity. If you say you're an executive coach, it's a pretty rare (and dysfunctional) person who will challenge you on it. If you act confident and clearly embody the person you want to be, you're creating a powerful feedback loop where people reinforce and validate your identity, and eventually that sinks in and you fully become what you want to be.

Embody Your New Brand

Sometimes one helpful secret, silly as it may sound, is to use props. The right outfit or context can dramatically affect your confidence and behavior. As leadership expert Warren Bennis recounts in his autobiography,

> During the war [WWII], being a soldier had considerable
> panache and came with an impressive costume—my
> handsome new uniform. And much as a good actor
> does, when I put on that uniform and the gold bars
> that went with it, I instantly became an officer in the
> U.S. Army. The role I stepped into prescribed certain
> attitudes and behaviors, and it also provided models
> for how I was to act. It empowered me to try on selves
> that nothing in my past had suggested to me. I was
> expected to lead my men and give and enforce orders
> and so I did, without any of the hesitation or insecurity
> that was natural to the boy I had been as a civilian. The
> uniform gave me permission—required me, really—to

observe the officers around me and to find potential strategies for being a successful officer in their example . . . in an almost magical way, the uniform seemed to bestow on me the ability to do what I had to do. It was talisman and inspiration, a symbol of my new authority and a mark of my new responsibility.[6]

Bennis isn't the only one susceptible to the power of a uniform; he recalls in his memoir how the film director Sydney Pollack told him that early in his career, he didn't know how to be a director, so he "tried to dress like a director—clothes that were kind of outdoorsy." Noted Bennis, "The role and a persuasive costume from L.L. Bean allowed Pollack to behave like a director until he truly became one."

The moral here isn't that you need military uniforms or safari vests to do your job. Rather, it's that everyone experiences a moment (or many moments) of doubt when they transition to a new role. The fastest way to overcome it is to throw yourself into your new identity with gusto. If a uniform (or a really nice new suit) helps, go for it. But do what it takes to present yourself with confidence, and that will inspire the confidence of others.

Developing a narrative that explains your transition may, to some, seem nice to have but not mandatory. After all, people will see your hard work and understand the direction you're going. Right? Unfortunately, though, many people can't or won't make the connections on their own. Until you make it explicit, they simply won't grasp how a helicopter pilot can succeed in business or how a poet can become a management consultant. It's your job to create a story so compelling, they can't help but understand and get onboard.

REMEMBER:

- ✓ Others will tune out if they don't understand the rationale behind your transition. Find a way to make the connections obvious between your past experience and your future goal.

- ✓ No one will care about or respect your rebrand if it seems like a narcissistic way to "find yourself." Make an effort to create a narrative that focuses on the value you can bring to others.

- ✓ Rebranding is a transition or a shift, not a Frankenstein full-body transplant. You can't go from cutthroat executive to Zen master without a few stops in between; it'll look phony and probably be phony. People can sniff out deception a mile away. The first rule of rebranding is to be true to yourself at all times.

- ✓ Believing in yourself is the first step. People won't take your new brand seriously if you act self-conscious or unsure of yourself. Even if it means "faking it till you make it," exude confidence so others will get the message.

CHAPTER 9

Reintroduce Yourself

Now that you've developed a compelling story that explains your transition, it's time to reintroduce yourself. People are busy, and it's often easier for your friends and colleagues to gloss over your hard work and stick to the same image of you they've always had. But, since we all rely on our networks for clients, connections, and job offers, it's up to you to ensure they understand that you've changed and grown, and their conception of you needs to change, as well. The secret is to orchestrate your "coming out" in the most memorable and strategic manner possible. In this chapter, you'll learn about:

- Why status is transferable and you *can* take it with you

- How to send the right signals

- How to shift your behavior to accord with your new image

- How to develop validators who can reinforce your new status

- Why you should go where the action is

- How to leverage symbolic actions to make an impression

Status—You *Can* Take It with You

It's a common frustration for professionals reinventing their careers: they've built up years of status and reputation in their initial field, and now it feels as if they're starting from zero as they enter a new domain. But Jeffrey Pfeffer, a professor at Stanford's Graduate School of Business and author of *Power: Why Some People Have It—and Others Don't,* says not to worry. "It's a psychological phenomenon known as the 'halo effect,'" he told me. "If I think you're good in one domain, I think you're going to be good in other domains, as well. There's the presumption that talented people have this set of generalized abilities."

In other words, your status is portable and transferable, which is why Hollywood actors are so often considered credible spokespeople on social issues, or why top business executives frequently win political office. That "durability of reputation"—across both time and situations—makes it essential for you to be strategic about how you're perceived from day one, says Pfeffer: "You need to do something to build a very good impression, a personal brand, and that will help you not only in your current place but in other places, as well."

The secret, then, is to leverage both your past experiences and the confidence that you've derived from your accomplishments. After all, other people take their cues from you, so when you're introducing your new brand, assume that others will welcome your contribution. That's the strategy Lisa, the legal scholar-turned-wine professional, took when she launched her new career path, and her self-assurance set the tenor of her interactions.

"I set out in a very positive manner; I was very optimistic," she says. "It was clear that I'm somebody who accomplishes things, and I could tell there would be somebody who'd want to talk to me." Her suspicions were correct. "Mostly I got respect," she recalls. "Wine is made to be sold, and you need to talk about it, be articulate, and be a self-starter, and it was clear that's what I was. Most people thought I had a lot of courage for making the choice I'd made." Today, she has a dream career leading advanced wine-tasting seminars, writing about wine, and consulting for foreign winemakers about how to position themselves in the American market.

Send the Right Signals

So, as in your initial self-inventory, take time to examine how you'd appear to others at all your "touch points." If you used to be a website designer but now want to do internet strategy, you should be sure to change the text on your website, your promotional materials, in your e-newsletter, and on various social media sites. (There are even more extreme cases where a "materials rebrand" is in order. Consulting expert Alan

Weiss tells a story about advising an aspiring business speaker whose efforts to be taken seriously by executives were thwarted by his use—and heavy promotion—of a talking puppet.)

Notes Cohn, the executive coach, "I notice that people have their own voices in their head and when they start making small changes, they think they look very significant to the outside world. But we only see your actions, what you say and do—all the wonderful insight and self-awareness you're getting, all the great ideas aren't affecting us. So it takes a lot to break through the noise, and you need to be hyperaware of what you're doing and make sure you're signaling explicitly to the outside world what you're trying to build."

Double-check everything; don't renew advertisements without reviewing the wording, and if you're giving a speech, print out a new bio for your introduction, just in case they pulled something old off the web. Even your phone greeting can be telling: does it reflect the impression you want? On a political campaign I advised, I forced one field organizer to change her voice-mail message, because "leave a message, I'll *try* to call you back" didn't exactly inspire confidence.

As you're launching a new brand, don't forget to proactively reach out by phoning or e-mailing your contacts—individually—to let them know about your new direction and, where appropriate, ask for their help, advice, or business. (Blast e-mails are a start, but too often go unread.) These are small steps, but because so much of what people know about you these days comes from online information, it's critical to keep it updated; it can lead to unexpected benefits, such as when a childhood friend of mine reconnected with me online, read my materials, and decided I'd be a perfect speaker for a conference she was organizing. Serendipity can happen if you're prepared.

You Don't Have to Say It—You Can Write It

No one likes a braggart, so it can be hard to find the right way to broadcast your accomplishments. But Robert Cialdini, the eminent psychologist and author of *Influence: The Psychology of Persuasion,* suggests two additional, subtle ways we can remind others about our new status or identities. First, we can leverage the written word. It turns out—for whatever quirk of culture—that you can get away with writing self-promotional things that you simply can't say in person.

"You have to do it in an indirect fashion," Cialdini told me. For example, if you're meeting with a professional colleague for the first time, he recommends that you "send a letter of introduction that says, 'I'm looking forward to our interaction on Thursday on the topic of X, and my background and experience with regard to X are as follows.'" Says Cialdini, "It's perfectly appropriate to say those things in a letter of introduction, but it's not appropriate as soon as there's a face-to-face interaction because you look like a boastful braggart and a self-aggrandizer." Since that's the case, you might as well leverage that opportunity and start making letters of introduction your standard operating procedure.

A second technique you can use, Cialdini suggests, is displaying your credentials so they're visible. He consulted for one hospital in Arizona that was struggling to get stroke patients to follow through with their home exercise regimen. When Cialdini began to investigate, he discovered something interesting: while the patients respected their doctors' expertise and credentials, they weren't being assigned the exercises by their doctors. Instead, physical therapy staff gave the assignments—"and we don't know anything about them."

Cialdini asked the head of the physical therapy unit to redecorate, putting up all the practitioners' credentials, diplomas, awards, and certifications, so patients could "see the evidence" of their competence. The result? "Exercise compliance jumped by 32 percent immediately," says Cialdini. "What I love about that is there was no burden involved. There was no cost, and the patients benefited, and so did the therapists, the hospital, the insurance companies. Nobody lost, and it was simply by raising to the surface something that was true but under the surface: the therapists' genuine authority."

Think about what strategies might work for you, whether they're introduction letters, diplomas in your office, or more information in your e-mail signature file. If the written word is a loophole through which you can better establish your expertise, it's incumbent on you to make use of it.

Shift Your Behavior

Small, tangible signals are only part of the battle, however. The biggest challenge is changing your behavior to reflect your new goals and reality. For over a decade, Dan had worked at a large, international technology company, ascending to the rank of engineering director. But when he decided to leave for a newer tech company with a hip reputation, he realized his résumé had some baggage attached. His previous employer was well-known and respected by the public, but in tech circles, it was viewed as an

old-line behemoth, resistant to change and full of stuffy bu-
reaucrats, not exactly the image he wanted to project to his
new colleagues. "I had to work to get other people to understand I was comfortable in the new environment," he says.
"It's a grassroots culture, so I had to start building relationships and trust. It was lots of time 'managing by walking
around,' being as visible as possible. With anything that
smacked of a big company, like having a standing staff meeting, I overreacted against it."

Dan realized he had to make connections quickly to shape
his colleagues' perception of him, but he was starting at a disadvantage. "I discovered my entire personal network was at
[my previous employer]," he recalls. "I decided I shouldn't be
in that situation again." So he embarked on a networking
campaign to deepen his connections both inside and outside
his new company, and in the process, build a reputation as a
forward-thinking, connected executive who understood industry trends. But there was only one problem: his personality. "I'm a fairly introverted guy," Dan says. "I hate taking
these meetings with strangers, the idea of a meeting that's
not going to help me get the job I have in front of me done,
or getting to know people without an action item."

But he forced himself to persist. "I realized it was important, that by the time you need connections, you can't suddenly
make them. You have to be ready." These days, while his
night-owl engineering team is sleeping in, Dan has a steady
regimen of breakfast meetings including "people in my industry at other companies, executive search people, leaders at
small companies, venture capitalists, a guy who works on corporate turnarounds." When it comes to making connections,
Dan says, "the biggest change is my default answer used to be

no, and now my default answer is yes. I've focused on reasons to say yes."

His networking has paid off. He's now on the pulse of start-ups to acquire and knows which ones are going down (and from which he can poach talent). He's made himself indispensable to his company and the furthest thing from an old school, bureaucratic manager. In fact, he's found ways to play with his background and upend expectations. When he discovered his new company required receipts for all travel expenses above $25, whereas his old firm's threshold was $75, he shook up his colleagues by letting them know it was less bureaucratic at his old company and suggested they change the policy. He recalls with pleasure: "I could use negative branding to my advantage." And he knows that if he wants to change jobs in the future, he's positioned himself with the contacts and branding he needs to land securely.

No Laughing Matter—How Al Franken Became Senator

Al Franken also had a branding challenge. He was certainly well-known, thanks to his years starring on *Saturday Night Live* and penning left-wing political humor books, including *Rush Limbaugh Is a Big Fat Idiot* and *Lies (And the Lying Liars Who Tell Them): A Fair and Balanced Look at the Right*. He'd proudly get into screaming matches with conservative talk show hosts like Bill O'Reilly. In the entertainment industry, controversy is good for business. But very different rules apply when you're running for elective office.

Franken's interest in politics had always been evident, and the Harvard grad clearly had intellectual chops (in 2003, his alma mater brought him back for a fellowship at the Shorenstein Center on the Press, Politics and Public Policy). But it was still a surprise in 2005 when the longtime East Coaster moved back to Minnesota, where he'd grown up, and started a political action committee called the Midwest Values PAC. The following year, he raised over a million dollars for Democrats across the country and made more than fifty appearances on behalf of Minnesota Democrats. And in 2008, in a

Try This

- Hire someone to spend a few hours combing through your touch points (voice-mail message, e-mail address, blog, website, social media accounts) to see if anything is off message. (It can simply be too hard for us to notice things ourselves.) He doesn't have to be a trained marketing professional, but you want someone reasonably smart and tech-savvy who can spot areas of dissonance for you.

- Go through your wardrobe. Is it appropriate? What would someone looking at your clothes surmise about you? If you're moving from start-ups into working for a law firm, you're going to need to upgrade to suits (and if your move is in the other direction, you don't want to be the only one in a necktie). In general, copy your prospective colleagues when it comes to the level of fanciness, but make the style your own.

- Make a list of three actions you can take in the next month to enhance your brand reintroduction (secure your own domain name, sign on to help with a major project, upgrade your work clothes, read more industry journals to become an information hub, and so on).

closely watched and hotly contested race, he was elected US Senator.

But it wasn't because of firebrand rhetoric or scathing humor at the expense of his opponents. In fact, on the campaign trail and once in office, Franken has used only the gentlest humor. And, recognizing the potential knocks against him based on his comedy career, he's bent over backward to demonstrate seriousness (securing funding for diabetes prevention and service dogs for veterans) and bipartisanship (his Senate bio is a veritable Republican love fest, giving shoutouts to his crew of GOP homies). Franken, like Dan, realized that to be viewed differently, you have to behave differently, in a consistent and visible fashion.

Develop Validators

Another important way we can convey our new identities is through external validators, that is, other people talking us up. As a powerhouse group of researchers led by both Jeffrey Pfeffer and Robert Cialdini discovered, the secret is to have someone else do the bragging for you. "People don't like people who self-promote," Pfeffer told me. "But ironically, even if you self-promote through the mouths of other people, somehow that stigma doesn't get associated with you. It's much better to have someone else toot your horn."

One possibility is to create a pact with a like-minded wingman to take turns promoting each other. This could take the form of him talking you up to colleagues, making juicy introductions at networking events ("You have to meet my friend Dorie; she has a new book out you'd love!"), or bringing up conversational topics where you excel.

Some people would view it as phony or shameless. I think that's exactly why you should do it. Too many people are missing a clear opportunity. After all, what's so wrong with consciously striving to promote the best attributes of your friend, and having him pique others' interest in you? At a minimum, it leads to better and more interesting conversations. And sometimes it can lead to powerful connections and business opportunities. Don't let a misguided sense of propriety keep you from leveraging such a valuable tool. Find a friend who's equally game, plan out the points you'd like each other to highlight (my new book, his new promotion), and start hitting the circuit.

What if you can't find a colleague who's willing to cross-promote? You might want to try Debra Feldman. She started her business, JobWhiz, in 2000 in order to help job seekers make career connections (she never promises that they'll find a job) for fees ranging from several thousand dollars up to $50,000, depending how labyrinthine their desired companies are to penetrate. Some clients simply don't have a lot of contacts, Feldman notes, because "their job is not to be a networker—it's a secondary part of their job." Others aren't sure of the best way to market or position themselves to prospective employers, and still others turn shy at the first roadblock or sign of rejection.

Feldman has no qualms aggressively promoting her clients: "I don't let any lead go. I always ask for the order, and if the contact is not interested, I'll almost always be able to get a referral. Whereas most people are really shy about asking for more help after they've been shot down, once I get a contact on the phone, I promote my client as someone they need to meet—not as a job candidate, but just giving them reasons to be intrigued. I'll cite a success story the person could relate to, or I'd tell them a personal experience I've had with that person that shows they're an outstanding individual . . . I have the patience to make it right."

But perhaps the most important advantage Feldman brings to her clients is the fact that someone besides them is making the sale. "There's an ascribed status to having another person involved in the transaction," she says. So whether you end up hiring a professional such as Debra Feldman to sing your praises or simply work out a deal with your friend, cultivating your own wingman can help break through the clutter and ensure the right people hear about your new brand.

Go Where the Action Is

As you're reintroducing your brand, you'll want to think strategically about your "unveiling." How can you grab people's attention and get them to take notice of your new identity? The last thing you want after investing so much time and energy into your rebranding is for people not to notice. Brainstorm about what affiliations or signs would be most powerful and meaningful to your target audience. Are there projects you can get involved with that will showcase your new interests and abilities or help you develop them? Organizational opportunities you can leverage (filling in for your boss while he's on paternity leave, transferring to the new office in China, or getting placed on a major client account)?

In general, you want to try to go where the action is— headquarters rather than field offices, departments that control budgets and decisions, or, simply, where your bosses are paying the most attention. During the 2004 presidential race, I worked for Howard Dean. That turned out to be a significant career advantage, since his campaign unexpectedly caught fire and dominated the headlines. But the people who benefited the most professionally were the folks who headed up our digital team, because blogs and social networking were new, sexy, and innovative.

The story line about the genesis of an "e-campaign" was irresistible to the media, which raised the profile of everyone involved in the effort and ensured it would be management's top priority. (I remember working late at night, waiting to consult with our internet-minded campaign manager, Joe Trippi, about an important statement to the press, while he repeatedly waved me off—"come back later!"—in order to spend more time working on a blog post.) Dean tech staffers formed several prominent online consulting firms after the campaign and, even as twenty somethings, were able to land blue-chip clients on the strength of the "Dean Internet" brand. Working on a signature initiative can serve as powerful shorthand for your mastery: if you can make it there, you can make it anywhere.

But what if you don't work for a prominent company or can't get onto the most desirable projects? (After all, competition can be tough for the most coveted spots.) Pfeffer, the Stanford business school professor, has good news for you. You can make a dramatic and visible impact even if you're the low man on the totem pole by identifying the opportunities you do have, but which most people overlook.

"A lot of routine, mundane tasks that most people wouldn't want to do actually bring you into contact with senior people in the organization," he says. "Often, small but important things aren't getting done—so when you do them, people will say, 'Wow, you took the initiative; that was very helpful.' And that will make people more familiar with you and your competencies and capabilities, and you'll build a much better image."

That approach worked for Heather, the transportation engineer, who cemented her relationship with the powerful leaders of her "women in transportation" committee by volunteering to serve as secretary. "I think I was always willing to take on the dirty work, the leg work," she recalls, while senior committee members were more interested in big-picture planning and networking. "As secretary, there wasn't a whole lot of glory, and there was a lot of work associated with it, like organizing logistics for meetings, but it gave me access to the inside scoop of how things happen—conversations that don't happen in public." She made herself indispensable while gaining an inside perspective that few others had.

Similarly, if you control resources of any kind, you can find a way to leverage them. Money is the obvious one. (Though, of course, you have to be mindful of both laws and propriety, as Massachusetts State Treasurer Tim Cahill found out when his office launched a $1.65 million advertising blitz for the Massachusetts Lottery, praising how well it was run—by him—just as he was running for governor. The state's attorney general was not amused.)

But information is another powerful resource. In the days before the internet was widespread, I worked for a newspaper that, astonishing as it now sounds, only had two internet-equipped computers. The reporters had to share them, and we'd hop on when we needed to look something up, and hop off (and back to our own, ancient computers) when it was time to do word processing. I had one colleague who would spend as much time as possible online and, when he'd come across a nugget, would scream it out across the newsroom and run in to tell our editor. She was thrilled and quite clearly considered him the best reporter on staff. Information was the currency of the newsroom, and he delivered.

Your job, then, is to figure out what currency you can traffic in, that matters to the people you need to influence. The information problem these days is different; there's simply too much of it to digest. So instead of racing across the newsroom to deliver an update, your competitive advantage will likely be in curating information—finding interesting intelligence that's been overlooked, or combining pieces of data and finding meaning in them. Whether it's creating a blog or e-newsletter that positions you as an informational hub, organizing a speaker series, or spearheading a cross-departmental initiative in your company, there are ways you can make connections, gain control of resources, and achieve visibility and prominence, even if you aren't starting from what others would recognize as an obvious base of power.

Leverage Symbolic Actions

One of the most important ways you can cement your personal brand and give it real meaning is to be on the lookout for symbolic opportunities. At the critical moment, are you standing up for what you say you believe? That was the question facing hospitality entrepreneur Chip Conley.

More than two decades ago, when he was only twenty-six, Conley purchased a rundown motel in a seedy part of San Francisco and launched his company, which he optimistically called Joie de Vivre. But despite its unlikely beginnings, he eventually grew it to become the second-largest boutique hotel chain in the United States. In the process, he developed the cornerstone of his management philosophy, which focused on creating an environment that allowed employees to feel comfortable and be themselves. It's a great sentiment. But to accomplish it, Conley decided he had to be the pacesetter. "If I can be honest, vulnerable, and authentic in my way of presenting myself inside my company and outside," he told me, "that's a helpful tool for others to understand that everybody goes through difficult times . . . The more we create a divide between the public image and the private reality, the more we create dysfunction."

He started by being open about his sexuality. "For gay men, it's an odd place in many corporations because the stereotype is they're weak and not competitive," he says. But he decided to use his identity as a source of strength. "Way before it was fashionable to be more emotionally open and empathetic as a senior executive, I've been doing it—partly because if you're gay or lesbian, you have to figure out how to walk into a room and make yourself comfortable in an environment where you feel like you're different. That helps you be empathetic to other people, to understand how it feels to be the other."

Conley also took the opportunity to stand up for self-expression in a very public way. After attending the Burning Man Festival one year (the popular, and sometimes wild, arts festival in the Nevada desert), he posted shirtless pictures of himself on Facebook wearing a sarong and a tutu. It didn't occur to him the pictures would be a big deal. They weren't obscene or even risqué, but they also didn't conform to the typical CEO image. Some senior members of his staff advised him to take them down. He said no.

"To take my pictures down in some ways is saying there's something wrong with me, that I should feel ashamed of what I did—and I don't," he told me. "Our mission statement is creating the opportunity to celebrate the joy of life, and that's what we were doing there." When a journalist heard the story and asked him to write a blog post about the controversy, it sparked worldwide attention. (He says the reaction was 80 percent positive, 20 percent negative.) "I just got to a place where I realized it was one more opportunity to be authentic in life. A lot of people said, 'We really appreciate the fact that you are who you are.'"

He believes that experience, and his overall emphasis on a culture of openness, pays dividends for Joie de Vivre. "Being authentic and vulnerable helps me, and it helps others be vulnerable with me," he says. "If you think your boss is above emotions, above having any difficult times . . . then that's going to make you feel like that's what you're going to have to be yourself. And if they feel like *I can't do that,*' it diminishes their ability to live up to their potential."[1]

Lots of companies pay lip service to the importance of "self-actualized employees" or an emotionally open environment. But Conley's experience shows the importance of bold, memorable gestures. It's why CEOs who are intent on creating change so often do things like rip out executive washrooms or sell off the company's art collection. In a multibillion-dollar corporation, one marble bathroom or Andy Warhol print isn't going to make much difference. But big, attention-grabbing symbols will stick in people's memory and influence their overall perceptions. A well-chosen gesture can come to define your entire brand, just as Conley's transparency came to embody Joie de Vivre.

As you fight, amid the bustle of everyday life, for your reinvention to be recognized, you want to choose the moments of greatest tactical advantage. You want to ensure your new identity is noticed. Maybe that means cultivating the right advocates and validators. Maybe it means ensuring you land on the right project team, or finding a hidden path to information or clout. It may even mean, like Chip Conley, realizing when your actions in a given moment will speak volumes about who you are and want to be. Most importantly, it means understanding that you can't simply tell others once about your new identity and assume they've now got it. Instead, your reinvention is an ongoing process and an ongoing opportunity to demonstrate who you are and what you can do best.

REMEMBER:

- ✓ Status often transfers between domains. If you've built up a reputation in one field, you may be able to leverage it in your new areas of interest (as seen with sports stars or financiers becoming politicians, or Hollywood stars becoming humanitarians).

- ✓ Think about unspoken ways to introduce your new brand and exude credibility. You can display diplomas or other awards in your office, send introductory e-mails before meeting someone citing your experience with a given topic, or use your e-mail signature file to convey important affiliations.

✓ Understand that the impression you're making may be different than what you think. Use trusted colleagues as a sounding board, because what matters is the message others are getting, not what you think you're conveying. Adjust accordingly.

✓ Making a pact with a colleague to talk each other up can be an important way to generate third-party validation for your new brand.

✓ Go where the action is. When in doubt, migrate to the parts of your company that control money, resources, or your leader's attention; you'll get noticed faster.

✓ Walk the talk. If you claim transparency and openness matters to you, be willing to share your unvarnished reality.

CHAPTER 10

Prove Your Worth

I've always been impressed with web or graphic designers. When they were job hunting, they could simply whip out their portfolio and show potential employers clear, concrete examples of their work. If the company liked the logos or websites or sample reports they saw before them, it was a go. But for most knowledge workers, the task was harder. How could you possibly demonstrate to an outsider what you're capable of? But with the internet, that's changed. Because there is zero cost to publishing your intellectual property, there is also zero excuse for not doing it. In this chapter, we'll talk about:

- Building your portfolio

- How to find the right medium for you

- Creating online relationships and how you can turn them into real-world connections

- How to keep social media from taking over your life
- Building your reputation in the real world

Building Your Portfolio

Developing your own content—that is, intellectual property—is a powerful tool for anyone. In fact, in a crowded marketplace where you're working overtime to establish your new brand, it's an essential strategy to showcase your knowledge and opinions, connect with interested parties (who are consuming your material), and establish an expert reputation (because the people who get cited and lead any industry's discourse are the ones who have a clearly stated, written philosophy). It's also the best way to overcome any objections you might face as a "brand reinventer." Your former colleagues may wonder how an oceanographer can become an investment banker, or how a tennis instructor can become a sales vice president, or how an engineer can become the head of human resources. This is your chance to let people judge you based on the quality of the material you produce, not on your past history or credentials.

After all, when someone comes to your website, he'll be regaled with compelling, thoughtful content that will dispel any doubts. Furthermore, you'll be e-mailing him relevant links ("Jeremy, I remember you were talking about your challenges with your sales team last month; here's a post I wrote that might be of interest"). You'll also be blitzing out your content via social media channels so that when anyone wonders what you're up to, the clear answer is "shaking up your new field."

A similar kind of content-fueled reinvention propelled Brian Clark (no relation) into an influential new career. Clark started the hugely popular website *Copyblogger,* which explains how to improve your website, and the sales that come from it, by creating better and more interesting content. *Copyblogger* has become a go-to tool for businesses and individuals seeking to turbocharge their online presence; *Advertising Age* ranked it third on its Power150 list of the most influential marketing blogs, and the *Guardian* named it one of the world's fifty most powerful blogs—period. So it makes perfect sense that it was started by . . . a lawyer? "I hated practicing law," Clark explained in an online interview, "and I was fascinated by the internet. The transition was extreme I suppose, but I always had a thing for writing, so I started creating online content over a decade ago. Now it's just part of me."[1]

His words are telling. Today, no one doubts Brian Clark's knowledge of online marketing. But flash back to a decade ago: wouldn't you be slightly suspicious taking advice from a random lawyer? So Clark walked the rebranding talk. He didn't immediately jump from the courtroom to pontificating about copywriting technique. Instead, he took time to learn and practice the skills he needed. He became a serial entrepreneur, building three offline businesses, but promoting them using the internet. In the process, he gained an understanding of what content most interested customers and how he should express it.

By the time he launched *Copyblogger* in 2006, Clark knew what would get people to click, and he's built a rabid following with a steady stream of posts on topics that obsess every online marketer, from "How to Get More Subscribers for

Your Email List" to "How to Write Headlines That Work." Clark gained the necessary skills and built a narrative for himself (lawyer to entrepreneur to online marketing expert). But most importantly, he built a portfolio for other people to see. Thanks to his *Copyblogger* posts, he's provided insight and value to others, while simultaneously marketing himself and his products to a swarm of eager customers.

If you're less tech-savvy, you may wonder about the feasibility of opting out of online branding in favor of more traditional methods. I'd say it's mandatory to pursue both channels; eschewing the online world can have serious unintended consequences. I once consulted for a client hiring a new senior executive, and the leading candidate was a man in his fifties who had worked for a number of years at a small firm. Amazingly, he had left so little of an online paper trail, my client became extremely concerned he was somehow faking his credentials and was only reassured after extensive conversations with his references.

Finding Your Medium

Blogging is one of the best ways to start getting your intellectual property out into the wider world. It's virtually free (you can pay for your domain name and hosting fees with Starbucks money) and doesn't require any fancy equipment or training; if you're pressed for time, you can pump out your posts at an airport lounge or on the commuter rail. But, admittedly, it's not the answer for everyone. Brian Clark always loved to write, and some of the best bloggers (like Andrew Sullivan, who runs "The Dish" for the *Daily Beast*) started life as journalists and are used to pumping out copy on deadline. But what if you're not much of a writer? In that case, you should make like Gary Vaynerchuk, an entrepreneur who turned his family's liquor store into an online empire through video blogging.

Vaynerchuk thought about creating a traditional blog, but writing wasn't his thing. If you're making a serious commitment to building your brand—and blogging, which requires regular and consistent updates, certainly qualifies—you don't want to choose a medium that fills you with dread, because you're going to fall off the wagon pretty quickly. After all, who wants to wake up every morning panicked about what to write that day? A blank screen can be pretty horrifying if writing doesn't come naturally. Just as fitness coaches advise you to pick an exercise you enjoy (I know I'll make it to the gym more often to play squash than if I'm forced onto a treadmill), you should find a way to express yourself that's fun and easy for you. In other words, play to your strengths.

That's what Vaynerchuk did in creating *Winelibrary.tv*. He's a passionate, charismatic speaker, which became a competitive advantage in the often-snooty wine world. He leveraged his natural talent and built up a following through consistency and hard work, posting a thousand daily web episodes until he retired the program in 2011.

Video blogging is an especially useful tool in building your brand through search engine optimization (i.e., scoring better in online search results). In 2006, Google purchased YouTube and, for obvious reasons, has been excited to promote video ever since. And now that broadband access is widely available, it's clear that online video is on a growth trajectory, with internet streaming eating the lunch of video rental chains like Blockbuster. To that end, Forrester Research discovered in

2009 that Google prioritized video over traditional text-based web pages—dramatically. In fact, videos were *fifty-three times* more likely to make it to the front page of a Google search.[2] So if you're looking to differentiate yourself and build a powerful brand on your chosen topic, making a lot of videos is a good start.

Fortunately, price is no longer a barrier. Most smartphones these days have high-definition video capabilities, extremely convenient if you want to film something interesting on the fly. For a sustained video series, however, you may want to invest in two items that will create a much better viewer experience. The first is a tripod (you can even purchase one specifically for your smartphone). Viewers can take a little shaking, especially if you're only producing a short snippet. But if you're planning an extended sit-down, you want to make it clear you're not recreating the *Blair Witch Project*. Buy a tripod that will hold the camera in place, give your arms a rest, and ensure a steady picture. The second is an external microphone (wireless ones are sometimes available, depending what kind of video camera you're using). The biggest "miss" of online videos is poor sound quality, which renders some—no matter how interesting their content—virtually unwatchable. You'll want to ensure people can hear what you or your interviewees are saying, and an external mic guarantees crisp sound.

Another worthy option for those who may not feel comfortable in front of a camera is to create a podcast series, which also has minimal start-up costs. You can certainly go all out and rent a recording studio if technical quality is essential to you. (One friend of mine runs a business creating podcasts for high-end musical groups who have to sound perfect.) But most of us won't require that level of investment. Three of my favorite techniques are recording a telephone interview with an interesting expert; monologuing into an external mic plugged into my computer; or simply recording one of my speeches to a crowd, such as a Chamber of Commerce or professional association. You can then edit the digital files using free software and put it online. To increase your visibility and make it easier for listeners to download, you can also make sure your podcasts are available via iTunes.

Your Multimedia Mix

If you're feeling especially creative, you can also try out a variety of multimedia options. That's been the approach of Dave Cutler, the aspiring marketer who got a mini-MBA at Rutgers and broadcast his job search via social media, winning coverage from the *Boston Globe* and local affiliates of Fox News and NPR for his use of such innovative techniques. "There's been a huge shift and the truth is, prospective employers are going to vet you through social media channels, whether you promote them or not," says Cutler. "It definitely behooves a job seeker to proactively enhance their profile through those channels so they reflect well on you. Plus, it's a way to demonstrate your knowledge, your creativity, and to add a little more personality."

Among his unique strategies, Cutler created his own smartphone app, which aggregates his blog, tweets, and videos—a treasure trove of information for any prospective employer. He also developed a "Dave Cutler's job search" venue on Foursquare, the location-based social networking site, that he checks into regularly. Because Foursquare focuses primarily on checking in to physical locations such as bars or restaurants, highlighting his job search is an intriguing surprise. "It's a channel that's a little quieter than Twitter," he says, so his message stands out. "I've had folks I'm connected to on Foursquare see it, and it's created potential leads."

Finally, he created video résumés that showcase his skills and personality. "The more you can show prospective employers who you are and demonstrate knowledge of the industry you want to work in, the better," he says. "They want to make sure it's an organizational fit and that your personality will fit in." He's noticed the videos can be an icebreaker, because employers have more information about him going in: "Last week I had a phone interview, and the interviewer said she watched my video and saw I have two little boys and a wife and a dog. She said, 'If you have a Little League game you need to go to, we're very understanding of that as long as you get your work done.'" As Dave's experience shows, creating good content and finding innovative ways to share it is still so unusual, it's a clear competitive advantage.[3]

Building Relationships Online

Another goal you can reach through creating content is networking and building relationships in your field. You can often interview top thinkers for your blog or podcast. It can be a challenge to break through the gatekeepers in celebrity-heavy fields like entertainment or sports, but generally speaking, if your industry's heavyweights aren't familiar to the general public, they're often accessible.

That's especially true if they're in the midst of promoting a book (their publisher doesn't want them to turn down a single opportunity to push sales) or, conversely, if it's a few years after the release of their best seller (because the number of media requests will have dropped precipitously). Interviews with thought leaders, insightful reviews of their books, or references to them in your work position you as a peer and someone worth getting to know.

A while back, I wrote a piece for the *Huffington Post* on "Why Your Personal Brand Shouldn't Be Your Corporate Brand." Toward the end of the article, I tossed out an example of strong personal branding from the ultimate productivity guru: "I can read *Getting Things Done* like everyone else," I wrote, "but I really want David Allen to come to my office and set up the system for me." Imagine my surprise when, a day or two later, David Allen himself e-mailed me his thanks. We've since phoned, e-mailed, and continue to keep in touch. More than you might imagine, people notice what you write, and creating good content sets you apart and gives people a reason to reach out.

So start making your list: who do you want to connect with in your industry? If you're a designer, for instance, how can you make friends with the dean of Stanford University's much-vaunted Institute of Design (aka "the d.school") or the head of IDEO? Read up on their past books and articles so you can reference them, note when they're releasing new works, and contact the publisher to request a review copy. And when you feel ready, request an interview, especially when they're on a publicity tour, and especially if they'll be in your city (in-person interviews obviously make a bigger impression in terms of relationship building). In a world of Cliff Notes and summaries typed up by interns, they'll be impressed you've read their work and have a thoughtful array of questions.

Finally, creating content helps you introduce yourself to new audiences. Posting content to your own blog is worthwhile, but it can be hard to attract a readership (most blogs are read by your mom, your best friend, and two people in Pakistan). Especially if you're focusing on a niche business topic, and unless you plan to plan to video blog in a bikini, your numbers are likely to be low. So how do you bolster your readership and become known outside your current circles? Two winning strategies are offering to guest-post on others' blogs and affiliating with well-known media outlets.

Finding Your Audience

If you've done enough research, you're probably familiar with the leading lights of your industry. Whose name is on everyone's lips? Who sets the tenor of the debate? Whose posts get people talking? Odds are, they too are under pressure to create a steady stream of interesting, provocative content, but, faced with a rowdy band of opinionated readers, their stress level is probably much higher. So come to their rescue. Familiarize yourself with their blog. See how long their average post is, and identify the topics that seem to galvanize their readers. Then reach out with an e-mail pitch and offer to help. Ramit Sethi, author of the best-selling *I Will Teach You to Be Rich,* is a huge advocate of guest-posting, noting in one article that his writing for Tim Ferriss's *4-Hour Workweek* blog and the popular *Get Rich Slowly* blog resulted in "hundreds of thousands of new readers, tens of thousands of new email subscribers, and thousands of books sold."

Sethi, who also accepts guest posts on his own blog, shares the following tips, which are applicable for almost any blog you'd like to crack into:

- Send a short, bullet-pointed list of ideas, which allows him to pick the topic most relevant to his readers.

- Include a link to writing samples (for this, you must already have your own blog), so he can make sure your literary chops are in order.

- Ensure your post is full of "research, charts, data, and expert quotes, not your opinion." Says Sethi, "It's easy to write what you think. It's much harder to produce data that backs up an argument."

- Make it easy for him by formatting your post correctly for his blog so it can be pasted in without additional work.[4]

Next, you'll want to explore the possibility of blogging or writing articles for prominent media outlets. Readers may not come to top business websites looking for you, but if they enjoy an article of yours they encounter, they're likely to visit your website, start following you on Twitter, or otherwise engage. Make a list of the publications that matter in your industry, see which ones feature pieces by outside contributors, and hone your pitch. (Industry trade groups are also frequently hungry for blog and newsletter offerings, and are a prime way to reach your target audience.) You'll have to be persistent—editors are usually overwhelmed by would-be contributors—but the exposure is worth the effort.

This strategy worked for Kathleen Kelley Reardon, a management professor at the University of Southern California's Marshall School of Business. Early in her career, she faced a challenge. Her expertise in business communication wasn't really respected by her traditional, data-obsessed colleagues who would determine whether she'd get tenure.

"I published in leading communication journals," she wrote in her book *It's All Politics: Winning in a World Where Hard Work and Talent Aren't Enough,* "but they were not the ones many business professors read . . . Yet insisting that journals in my field were just as good as those respected by

Try This

- Create a list of potential blog topics and keep it updated as new ideas occur to you. You can start your list by thinking about the questions people most often ask you about your field, the impact of new technology, the things most people don't understand or get wrong about your field, success secrets you've observed in your industry, and so on.

- Make a list of at least a half-dozen publications that matter in your industry. Go online and look up the name and address of their online editor. Make a note in your calendar to contact them in three months, after you've built up a good set of clips from your own blog, to approach them with a pitch.

- Schedule your social media. Spend a couple of weekend days pounding out content, so you have a backlog. Schedule your posts to load at predetermined intervals to take the pressure off; if you get slammed at work and miss a week or two, you have enough material to keep you covered.

finance professors or complaining that promotion criteria were skewed and unfair would not have helped. What I needed to do was raise my value to the Marshall School." So she embarked on a campaign to break into *Harvard Business Review* and other top business journals her colleagues valued, and to write books that received significant publicity. Her strategy worked and, despite her colleagues' initial reluctance, she became a tenured professor.

How to Keep Social Media from Taking Over Your Life

When I give talks, one of the most frequent questions from aspiring brand builders relates to the frequency of posting. How much is enough? And how can you keep social media from taking over your life? (It would certainly be easy to spend every waking minute "liking" things on Facebook and monitoring the endless flow of tweets.) Gary Vaynerchuk became famous for his dedication to responding to every fan e-mail; his first book, *Crush It!*, attributes his success to staying up all hours of the night writing comments on people's blogs, cross-posting his videos everywhere on the web (not just on popular sites like YouTube), and literally building his fan base one person at a time. So do you have to give up your life to the flickering blue light? Not necessarily.

Tim Ferriss certainly doesn't. In fact, he posts on his extremely popular blog once or twice a week at best; often there's nearly a two-week delay. Why? He believes posting less frequently actually helps his blog. "It allow comments to accumulate," he explained in an interview with the website *ProBlogger,* "which reinforces the perception that your blog is popular. It also offers you the breathing room to focus on quality, which creates the popularity and stickiness. People have a lot of crap information being forced upon them, so I only want to add a good dash of fun and education when I have something worthy to say . . . Last but not least, it takes a while for posts to propagate through the web, and most people simply track back to your most recent post, so leaving a post up for a few days in pole position has been an important tactic for me."[5]

Marketing guru Seth Godin posts seven days a week, but not because he thinks that's a magic number. Rather, he told *Advertising Age,* "I find that I have about six bloggable ideas a day. I also find that writing twice as long a post doesn't increase communication, it usually decreases it. And finally, I found that people get antsy if there are unread posts in their queue. Hence, the compromise on daily."[6] As both Ferriss and Godin indicate, you should only post as frequently as you have high-quality material to share. My general advice to clients is that they should post often enough to keep people coming back (so their blog doesn't appear abandoned), but not so much that it becomes an unbearable chore—for you or your readers. Generally, that means picking a frequency somewhere between once a day (at the high end) and twice a month (at the low end), with most people clustering around one to three times per week.

Scheduling Your Way to Sanity

The other strategy that's saved me from madness is scheduling tweets in advance using a service like TweetDeck or Hootsuite. Some might argue that scheduling tweets is anathema to Twitter's ethos of real-time interaction—diving into the stream and retweeting interesting stories, direct messaging your contacts, interacting with fans, and responding to the news of the day. That's nice to do sometimes to keep things lively, and it's an important element if you choose to make social media ubiquity your exclusive marketing strategy, as Vaynerchuk did. But it's just not practical for most people all the time. Anyone who reads productivity books knows that Twitter is a black hole that can easily suck you into its vortex, so you must have a plan.

As with blogging, I encourage my clients to have a baseline presence on Twitter, which shows that you're engaged and keeping up with the times. But unless it's so much fun for you that it becomes your hobby of choice, you should seek to minimize your time spent on it. Shoot for one to two posts per weekday and you'll look perfectly respectable; even more is better, but there can be too much of a good thing: the people who blast things out five hundred times a day are impressive but also risk annoying the daylights out of their followers. Here are the steps to a painless Twitter presence:

- Block out an afternoon on your calendar to brainstorm a list of tweets (i.e., one- to two-sentence nuggets of wisdom). I can often bang out a hundred to two hundred in a couple of hours. These should be tips, insights, or recommendations that establish your expertise in your chosen field (not the oft-mocked "Just bought my Egg McMuffin"–type posts). Some examples from my Twitter feed—which focuses on marketing, branding, and business strategy—include:

  - How to create buzz? Think about marketing as you design a product, not after.

— Have you had coffee with your local reporter? If not, invite them today.

— Can everyone in your organization clearly state your mission? Test them.

- Set up your scheduling account and schedule your posts a month in advance, so you don't need to worry about what you should write on any given day. (It's hard to think of a worse use of your time than stressing out about what 140-character post you're going to send on a given day when you're facing meetings, deadlines, and actual work.)

- Once a day, for five minutes, visit your scheduling account to see if you need to respond to any messages. You can also scan the feed of the folks you're following (ideally, thought leaders you'd like to emulate and connect with in your field) and retweet interesting material. (Keep retweeting enough and you're likely to get on their radar screen, especially if they're not yet in the superstar category, with hundreds of thousands of followers. Along these lines, a nice Twitter tradition is "Follow Friday," in which you give a shout-out each week to Twitter feeds you think are particularly worth recommending to others.) You can also use this daily check-in to update your queue of posts and add in links to new blog posts you've written. If you find yourself losing track of time and can't keep to the five-minute limit, stick to visiting your scheduling account three times a week; waiting a day to respond to a message usually won't kill you.[7]

Capture That Data!

The other important thing to consider in ensuring that social media doesn't take over your life is that you need a system for capturing ideas so that when *Forbes* asks you to write a guest post, you're not banging your head against a wall trying to come up with content. Here are some of my strategies:

- Capturing ideas in my smartphone. If you're paying attention, just living your life will give you plenty of ideas. During a fruitless quest to buy socks in midtown Manhattan, I dreamed up an idea for a post on "the limits of serendipity"—that is, sometimes you want to browse around, wander, and be exposed to new things . . . and other times you just want to buy your socks, so you need to set up systems that allow you to be efficient when you need to. I probably would have forgotten all about it once my blood pressure went down and my rage at Macy's bizarre store layout subsided. But instead, thanks to a note I recorded on my phone, I can now channel it into a blog masterwork. (Apparently, I'm not the only one who files ideas on an iPhone; *The New Yorker* reports pop singer Taylor Swift likes to capture melodies as voice memos.)

- Keeping an idea file. Keeping ideas in your phone or calendar is great for a while, but eventually you'll lose track. That's why, every few weeks, I transfer my new ideas into a master file called "Blog Topics." It now clocks in at forty-seven pages and will likely provide enough ideas to keep me writing into retirement.

- Start with the title. Still having trouble coming up with a winning idea? Starting with the title can often help you structure your post and ensure you stay on topic. Brian Clark of *Copyblogger* suggests "The Cosmo Headline Technique for Blogging Inspiration." Pick up a copy of *Cosmo*—which has perfected the art of irresistible headlines—and adapt them for your purposes. "The 22 Best Relationship Tips Ever" becomes, in Clark's telling, "My 22 Best Design Tips Ever." Meanwhile, "Guys Spill: White Lies They Tell Women All the Time" morphs into "Realtors Revealed: The Little White Lies We Tell Clients (And How to Stop)."

Building Your Reputation in the Real World

Curating your online presence is extremely important because more people are going to follow your life and career developments online than in person (you may have a thousand Facebook friends, but you're never going to have time to have coffee with each of them and explain your new career aspirations). Sometimes that online light touch is fine; after all, as Stanford sociologist Mark Granovetter famously discovered in his study of the "strength of weak ties" (popularized by *The Tipping Point*), more people find jobs through acquaintances than friends, because casual connections can plug them into networks and information they wouldn't otherwise have access to. But to ensure your new brand spreads widely and deeply, you can't rely on online methods alone.

So what steps can you take to demonstrate your chops in real life? One of the best, suggests the consulting expert Alan Weiss, is to get involved with your field's professional association. It helps you make connections with other practitioners (always good for referrals, in case they can't handle a particular assignment) and ensures you're staying on top of the latest thinking and best practices. But even more than that, says Weiss, it provides an opportunity to build visibility among your peers and beyond. In the mid-1990s, he agreed to serve as the president of the National Speakers Association's New England chapter. "I thought I'd do less business those years," he told me, because with his association commitment he'd have less time available to seek out new clients. "But to my surprise, I did about $250,000 more business. The visibility naturally accrues to you, and even though you don't seek it out, people come to you for interviews and advice. Your visibility grows and your brand grows."

The secret, which most people don't realize, is that they should aggressively seek out a leadership role. "My advice to people today," says Weiss, "is if you're going to join a trade or professional association—any volunteer association—it's 'in for a dime, in for a dollar.' Take some kind of leadership position, lead a committee, head a task force, be an officer, but don't just sit there week after week." While most of your peers are halfheartedly attending meetings or trading business cards at the back of the room, you can become a connector and power broker—knowing everyone, and at the center of the action. Leading the group means you not only have an excuse to talk to anyone, but they're simultaneously seeking you out.

Start Your Own Group

What if your trade association or Chamber of Commerce is boring, hidebound, or led by an impenetrable cabal from the old boys' network? Start your own. It takes more work and entrepreneurial ambition to convince others to spend their time on your start-up, but, if you can convince them the networking and content value is sufficient, the payoff is also much greater. The World Economic Forum, which sets the international business agenda each year with its January conference in Davos, Switzerland, wasn't created from on high. A business school professor from Geneva, Klaus Schwab, got the idea and made it happen. Now he's a lot more powerful than most CEOs, whose companies pay tens of thousands of dollars in membership fees to be part of the club. (The forum's annual budget now tops $100 million per year.)

A smaller-scale, but still powerful, example is Chris Brogan, a well-known blogger and coauthor of the best-selling *Trust Agents: Using the Web to Build Influence, Improve Reputation, and Earn Trust*. (You may also remember him as Dave Cutler's job search booster.) Brogan didn't start out with unusually grand connections or credentials. In fact, he was a college dropout working as a project manager at a telecom company: your average geek, who took an early interest in blogging and podcasting. Today, with hundreds of millions of blogs, it's harder to build up an audience. But as an early and committed adopter, Brogan built up a following for his regular posts, many of which sought to explain the new social media phenomenon and the best ways to leverage it. He also embraced the idea of an online community and became tight with many other bloggers (who, in linking to his posts, further amplified his brand).

In 2006, when Brogan co-organized a gathering called PodCamp Boston "where newbies and advanced content makers alike come to learn more about and share their knowledge of podcasting, blogging, video blogging, social media, and more," it solidified his reputation as a leader and authority in these emerging fields. And when the PodCamp concept went viral and expanded to other cities like Pittsburgh, San Francisco, Atlanta, and Copenhagen within less than three months of the original event, it exposed literally thousands of other content producers to Brogan's ideas and philosophy (who could then blog and tweet about it). Today, Brogan consults for *Fortune* 500 companies and makes a healthy living as a professional speaker, bringing in (as of late 2011) $22,000 a pop.[8]

The Joy of Public Speaking

Which brings us to another superb way to establish your credentials in your new realm: public speaking. Giving talks clearly isn't for everyone; if the prospect makes you shudder, it might be worth a few visits to Toastmasters to overcome your anxiety, but you probably don't want to make it the cornerstone of your marketing (why suffer?). But if speaking is actually fun for you, then it represents the best win-win possible.

First, it gives you an opportunity to interact with an entire room full of prospective clients (or, at least, recommenders) in an expert capacity. The biggest challenge for any professional who traffics in ideas is that it's often hard for potential clients to evaluate their merits. Are you a good lawyer? I'm not sure; I can't really evaluate that since I haven't been to law school. Are you a good marketing strategist? How can I possibly tell until I've already hired you and see what you come up with? There's a tremendous fear of buyer's remorse; after all, clients or potential employers will be shelling out thousands of dollars (or more) for an uncertain outcome. But seeing you speak is a quick way to alleviate those fears because they're able to see you in action, interact with you in real time (via Q&A or chatting with you afterward), and get a sense of what you'd be like to work with. That's something Twitter simply can't provide, no matter how witty your repartee.

Second, your credibility is enhanced from the get-go by the implicit endorsement of the host organization. The Chamber of Commerce or local Rotary or the Southwestern Association of Cattle Ranchers wouldn't bring you in to address their members if they didn't think you had something worthwhile to say. So there's a lower barrier for the organization's members to accept you as an expert (and, in turn, to hire you for further speaking or consulting services).

Third, speaking provides you with an opportunity to leverage your content. In addition to the people you're reaching in the room that day, you also have the ability to:

- Record your remarks. You can turn them into a podcast or possibly a CD or download you can sell.

- Attract media attention. You can invite the local newspaper or TV station (local access television is often desperate for good content to film).

- Provide additional content to organization members. You can provide a white paper as a handout and offer to let the organization reprint it in its newsletter, which is how I ended up being featured in such unlikely (but excellent) venues as the newsletter for the New Hampshire Association of Chamber of Commerce Executives and *QRCA Views,* the magazine of the Qualitative Research Consultants Association.

Getting Yourself Booked

In short, public speaking is a powerful, efficient way to market yourself and your new brand (and, as with Brogan, if your profile becomes sufficiently robust, you may even get paid to do it). The obvious way to book speaking engagements is to work with a professional speakers' bureau. Unfortunately, however, they primarily want to work with celebrities or professionals whose brands are so well-known that the speaking engagements practically sell themselves. If you're just beginning to establish your new brand, you'll probably need to do the marketing yourself. To get some experience under your belt (and rack up testimonials and perhaps sample video clips), start small and local. Your Chamber of Commerce and Rotary are usually good bets; they often need speakers and, because they don't pay, are more willing to take risks in booking new talent.

Eventually, you'll work up to speaking to regional or national trade associations: a target-rich environment for clients or potential employers. To learn more about how to break in, check out Alan Weiss's excellent *Money Talks* and *Million Dollar Speaking,* and pick up a copy of Columbia Books's *National Trade and Professional Associations Directory* (or, even better, look for it at the library, because it costs several hundred dollars). Writing an inquiry letter citing your credentials and the amazingly relevant talk you can give to their members can sometimes get you in the door, but the very best bet is to drill down into your existing clients, friends, and contacts. What associations and organizations are they involved with? Who can they introduce you to?

A "warm" lead is far more likely to result in a successful booking, which is how I've ended up speaking at conferences such as the Association for Commuter Transportation International Conference (a client who was a member suggested me) and the National Lesbian and Gay Journalists Association International Convention (the brother of a former colleague was that year's program coordinator). In short, if you enjoy public speaking, this is one of the best ways to broadcast your new brand and expertise widely.

REMEMBER:

✓ Getting involved in social media really isn't optional anymore. If you're reinventing yourself professionally, you need to establish a powerful online identity that demonstrates your expertise, and social media is a critical tool.

✓ The return on investment for social media isn't always apparent. You may generate immediate sales from a blog you wrote or tweet you sent, but it's not likely. Instead, the effect is aggregate and builds over time. It's your calling card, and that takes time to build.

✓ It's your pick whether your blog is text, video, or audio (i.e., a podcast), or all of the above. The trick is to find a medium you're comfortable with and create content consistently.

✓ Look at your online brand building as networking on steroids. You have the ability to connect with prominent people in your industry and potential clients (by interviewing them, writing blog posts that mention them, commenting on their blogs, retweeting their material, etc.) and to create content that draws them to you.

✓ Leverage your content creation. Start with your own blog, and then—once you've built up sample clips—consider writing for other outlets (magazines' websites, the blogs of other popular writers) to increase your audience reach.

✓ Social media can quickly become overwhelming. Use online tools (such as Hootsuite or TweetDeck) to schedule your posts in advance and respond to messages at predetermined times.

✓ Don't forget that both online and offline brand building are necessary. Seek out a leadership role in industry groups, begin public speaking, and consider starting your own organization so you can raise your profile and become a connection hub.

CHAPTER 11

Keep It Going

I recently gave a talk at a leading business school, and afterward a student sidled up to me with a question. "How long," he asked, "does it actually take to reinvent your personal brand?" There's no easy answer, of course. It depends on the extent of your change and the depth of your previous reputation. (It's a lot easier for a junior executive to rebrand himself as a team player than it would be for someone like Larry Summers, the famously querulous economist and former US Treasury Secretary.)

Reinvention never happens overnight. Even if it's possible to wake up and be a different person, other people simply won't believe you until you demonstrate that change over time. A quick change, followed by a reversion to past behavior, looks like a manipulative feint, and that can actually damage your reputation in the long run. But reinvention also doesn't have to be a thankless and eternal slog. While it's true that we "reinvent ourselves every day," in this book, I'm positing that you start at Point A (your current brand) and, with the right planning and execution, do eventually end up at Point B (how you want to be perceived moving forward).

"You probably won't be able to convince anyone you've changed in less than three months," I told the student. "For relatively small changes, you can manage them in a few months by consistently demonstrating your new behavior. For larger ones—especially career shifts where you may need to gain new skills or go back to school—it'll take a few years. It's hard work, but it's not a lifetime. You're going to be a few months or a few years older, anyway, and you might as well position yourself for the success you want." So how do you ensure that you're moving forward in the right direction and keeping your brand momentum going? In this chapter, we'll talk about:

- Why it's essential to monitor your brand and make adjustments where necessary

- How to keep yourself from backsliding into your old identity

- Why you shouldn't be afraid to reevaluate

- The importance of staying consistent and following your path

Monitor Your Brand

It's the butt of jokes: the narcissist who sits at his computer, endlessly Googling himself to see what comes up. "Oh, I never do that," some people aver. What a shame. Not only is it a good idea to do an online inventory of yourself, as we suggested in chapter 2, but you're also going to want to create a Google Alert for yourself, which will e-mail you anytime an article or blog post mentions your name. There are fancier and more expensive systems available to track what's being said about you, but unless you're a celebrity who's constantly being assessed in the media, Google's no-cost alert system will do just fine.

Most of the time, you may not get any hits at all. But in the event that someone does mention you, it's critically important for you to know. That way, you can thank someone for a kind mention or flattering portrayal and immediately correct any negative or incorrect information before it has time to spread. Similarly, you'll want to keep an eye on Twitter. Using a service like Hootsuite or TweetDeck, you can easily (and again, for free) track online mentions and respond in a timely fashion.

But tracking online perceptions isn't everything. Sometimes, you need the curated perspective of real people to help you make sense of the data. In the popular TV show *Mad Men,* set in the chic advertising world of the early 1960s, there's a scene in which ad man Freddy is suggesting concepts for Pond's Cold Cream, which they're trying to sell to younger women: *How about Jessica Tandy as a spokeswoman? How about Doris Day? Tallulah Bankhead?* He goes through a list of aging stars that leaves Peggy, a young female exec, exasperated. Younger women don't look to older, fading stars for beauty tips, she explains. Freddy is needling and insistent, and an offended Peggy finally blurts out the truth: everyone in the office considers him "old-fashioned"—the kiss of death in an industry that prides itself on being cutting edge.

No one wants to be Freddy, oblivious to his reputation until someone gets angry and mouths off. So how can you keep on top of perceptions and ensure your rebranding is taking root? Think back to the people you may have consulted for your personal 360—friends and colleagues who care about you and know you well. If they seemed receptive to sharing feedback about you and your performance, this could be a good way to keep them engaged and involved in your life, *if* they bring a positive, action-oriented perspective (one telltale sign is how hard they work to improve themselves). Next, think about other people in your company or industry whom you respect. Who's a connector (but not a gossip)? When you've identified a small group of people whom you think would be a good fit, ask if they'd be interested in periodically touching base to share ideas. Shoot for only three or four, because you only want advice from the most perceptive people you know.

With a smart, savvy group of advisers looking out for him, *Mad Men*'s Freddy could have picked up early warning signs he was viewed as old-fashioned and taken steps to prevent that. Similarly, with your kitchen cabinet scanning the horizon for threats and opportunities, you'll be the first to know if trends are changing or your reputation stumbles and will be able to quickly steer it forward.

After all, sometimes a quick fix can make all the difference. Rebecca Zucker, the executive coach, recalls that one of her clients, an attractive female management consultant, had a problem everyone was afraid to talk to her about. "It was her makeup, her hair, her jewelry," says Zucker. "Her shirts would be too low cut. She wasn't portraying the sophisticated professional I think she'd prefer." When she finally learned the truth and made a few simple changes, her career thrived.

Make a Public Commitment

But what if the changes you need to make are harder than simply buying a more discreet wardrobe? It's possible you might find yourself falling back into old patterns you had hoped to change. In that case, consider enlisting accomplices who can encourage you on the right path.[1] The best way to leverage the influence of those friends and colleagues is by making a public commitment.

Brian Stelter was a hotshot reporter with a dream job. His independent blog covering the TV news industry became so popular that he was recruited to cover television and the web for the *New York Times*. But all those hours sitting in front of a computer and monitoring the flicker of news updates had taken their toll: at only twenty-four, he had ballooned to an unhealthy 270 pounds. An expert at new media, Brian decided to use familiar tools to his advantage. "I knew that I could not diet alone," he wrote in August 2010. "I needed the help of a cheering section. But rather than write a blog, keep a diary, or join Weight Watchers, I decided to use Twitter." His initial plan was to lose twenty-five pounds in twenty-five weeks by publicly blasting updates like "Last nite: asparagus sted of fries, but too much alcohol. Today: fruit; then sushi, little bit of soy sauce, 1 cookie sted of usual 3." Inspired by the six hundred followers who eventually signed on, he reached his goal and then decided to lose an additional twenty-five pounds before his twenty-fifth birthday. He eventually powered down to less than two hundred pounds using his unique calorie-tracking method.

Keep from Backsliding

Keeping a public promise is one way to motivate yourself to stay in line. Another is avoiding the loss of money. That's what three Yale professors discovered when they founded the website stickK.com (yes, with two "k's"). Dean Karlan, an economics professor, became intrigued with the idea of opening a "Commitment Store" to help people stick to their promises by making public contracts, with financial consequences attached. "The Commitment Contract concept is based on two well-known principles of behavioral economics," the stickK.com website explains. "1. People don't always do what they claim they want to do, and 2. Incentives get people to do things."

Karlan's first test was his own. Like Stelter, he and a grad school friend were disturbed about their steady weight gain, so they decided to make a pact with profound consequences. If either failed to lose the promised amount of weight (their goal was thirty-eight pounds apiece), they would forfeit *half of their annual salary*. Though there were a few hitches along the way— learning, for instance, that they had to make the contracts non-negotiable so they wouldn't let each other off the hook—they both eventually lost the pounds. And they kept up the commitment to maintaining their weight: "At one point, my friend bounced up a bit, so he had to pay me $15,000," Karlan writes. "This payment was an investment in his ongoing health. Had I refused to accept it, no future contracts would ever work."

Today, Karlan still keeps up an ongoing commitment contract with another colleague to the tune of $1,000 per week if he starts gaining weight. When the stakes are high enough and the humiliation public enough, it can become easy to do

> ## Try This
>
> - Make a list of your most "with it" friends and colleagues. Reach out to three to six of them and ask if they'd like to get together periodically to trade ideas. Schedule a meal with at least one of them, once a month, to keep yourself fresh.
> - Is there a key behavior you need to adopt (weight loss, finally learning a new language, getting to work on time)? Make a public commitment and a pledge so hard it hurts—a $1,000 fine for a minor infraction will get you moving in the right direction fast.

the right thing. Indeed, as of this writing, stickK.com featured well over a hundred thousand pledges and had over $8.3 million in bets on the line; many goals had direct business implications, ranging from a pledge to "cold call 120 businesses per week" to "get to work before 9:30 every day" to "no snark or uncalled-for negativity." Making any of those changes would be likely to improve your career.

Don't Be Afraid to Reevaluate

You're in the thick of your new professional identity. You're creating content, you're monitoring your new brand, you've got your kitchen cabinet—and you're miserable. What should you do?

Life is too short. It may be time to reinvent yourself yet again or to go back (perhaps in a new form) to your old identity. You should never be afraid to reevaluate your choices and your options. That's what happened with Tom Benner, who lost his job as a newspaper reporter after more than twenty years in the business. "Did I see it coming?" he asks. "No. Should I have seen it coming? Maybe." In truth, he felt insulated; he'd risen to a prestigious bureau chief post, and he loved his work: "Covering live news, reporting on it that day, the adrenaline of a deadline, writing for a broad audience, getting information out to people—that's what journalism is all about."

But newspapers were an industry in decline. The Project for Excellence in Journalism estimates that a third of American newspaper reporters lost their jobs in the 2000s (indeed, I was one of them), and TV network news staffs have been cut by half since their 1980s peak.[2] It was hard for Tom to give up a career path where he had found fulfillment and professional success. He tried freelancing for a few months, but it couldn't compare to his previous income. Finally, he decided to bite the bullet; he got a job as a communications director for a nonprofit. "I kept saying to myself, I'll give it a shot, this is what people do—they get serious jobs."

Tom was still able to enjoy parts of his job that carried over, like writing reports and crafting op-eds. And he was glad to pick up social media skills in his new position. But the passion never kicked in for him, so after three years, he decided to quit: "I didn't feel like I was doing what I loved to do and what I was best at."

Somehow, he had to get back to journalism. There was no returning to the pre-internet glory days, when Sunday papers were so filled with ads that lifting one could give you a hernia. But he did find a meaningful opportunity, becoming the part-time editor of a local newspaper written and sold by homeless people as an alternative to panhandling. "People who are smart get out of the newspaper industry," he admits ruefully. But he just couldn't help himself: "Our newsroom is in the basement of the Old Cambridge Baptist Church. It's not the *Boston Globe,* but I still get a thrill that makes things worthwhile."

Even when we research and strategize, it's always possible that our new direction might not be a fit. Is it fun to go to work? Do you feel like you're making progress in your life? Are you doing what you want to do? If not, it's important to be open to that realization. Cultivating a brand is important, but it has to be a brand you truly embrace. It's not easy to admit mistakes, but doing so early can save you a great deal of trouble.

I have a friend who left her lucrative database programming job to go to culinary school and even moved to another state for her studies. But after a year and a grueling internship that involved getting to work by 3 a.m. to start baking, she realized databases weren't so bad after all. A year of culinary school wasn't cheap, and she doesn't have a degree to show for it. Then again, it's clear she doesn't want to be a professional chef, and now she has the time and luxury of baking bread when she pleases. So be honest with yourself and don't be afraid to reevaluate your strategy where necessary.

Be Consistent

One of the most important ways you can maintain your positive brand momentum is to be consistent. You want people to feel they understand who you are, where you're coming from, and the nature of your trajectory over time. What you don't want to do is look like an opportunist, a brand problem that tripped up one notable young entrepreneur.

Let's imagine, for instance, that you founded an extremely well-known company. And let's imagine someone wrote a semifictionalized book alleging that you stole the idea for it and then cheated your best friend out of billions of dollars. Now let's imagine there's going to be a movie adaptation of that book, which will be seen around the world. So the week before it comes out, it would be a really good idea to announce that you're giving away $100 million to charity, right?

Actually, no. As you may have guessed, we're talking about Mark Zuckerberg, the controversial hoodie-clad billionaire who was profiled in the Oscar-winning film *The Social Network*. A son of wealthy Westchester County, New York, parents, he had no connection to hardscrabble Newark, New Jersey. But apparently, after meeting the city's charismatic mayor at a conference a couple months before, he was moved to fork over $100 million to improve the city's public schools.

It would be churlish to criticize a massive charitable gift that Zuckerberg didn't have to make, and it's apparently only the start, as he's signed on to Bill Gates and Warren Buffett's Giving Pledge, which stipulates that he'll give the majority of his wealth to charity. But from a public relations perspective, it was awful timing, appearing like a cynical ploy to divert attention from a negative story. Even if you're spending $100 million to help a good cause, you can still look inauthentic if you appear to be acting for the wrong reasons. You can't buy goodwill—even with hundreds of millions of dollars—when you're in crisis. Instead, you need to build it up over time.

Build Up Goodwill

Perhaps the antithesis of Zuckerberg's quick-fix attempt at rebranding is Howard Dean's hard work and consistency, which paid major political dividends for him, his reputation, and his political party. You may remember Dean as the former

Vermont governor who soared to unprecedented popularity in the 2004 presidential race, only to crash and burn at the Iowa caucuses. As Dean's New Hampshire communications director, I had an up-front look at him and his campaign.

Dean genuinely wanted to reform American politics. He despised the closed-door calculations that wrote off entire parts of the country as "unwinnable" for Democrats and therefore cut off party resources (a situation that would only lead them to become more unwinnable in the future). He delighted in the national excitement his campaign was generating and, thanks to a new generation of online tools like blogs, we were able to engage not just people in Iowa and New Hampshire (the early primary states that get disproportionate love from political candidates) or major donors. Instead, regular voters eagerly got involved, holding Meetups across the country.

But all that ended in January 2004 on the day of the Iowa caucuses. Battered by an unceasing cavalcade of negative ads funded by pseudo-independent groups tied to our Democratic opponents (and quite likely hobbled by our campaign's faulty strategy to bring in energetic non-Iowans to volunteer, thereby alienating actual Iowans), Dean finished a distant third. The campaign didn't end that night; it sputtered on for another month. But it couldn't overcome the puncturing of Dean's front-runner status and, even more importantly, the iconic "Dean Scream," which aired nonstop on cable television. (During Dean's concession speech, in which he vowed to keep fighting on in other states, he had to yell to be heard above the crowd. The TV cameras only picked up his microphone, not the background noise, so he appeared to be psychotically shouting for no reason at all, an unfortunate image for a potential commander-in-chief.)

When Howard Dean dropped out of the presidential race, it would have been easy to skulk back to Vermont or head to a tropical island. He'd come so close to victory, but had left humiliated, mocked by every smug anchor on television. I would have understood the temptation; I couldn't bring myself to move on to John Kerry's campaign (the eventual nominee) and instead took a job running a nonprofit. But Dean stayed focused on his goal of building a strong Democratic Party. He gamely campaigned around the country for Kerry, despite Kerry operatives' leading role in producing the vitriolic ads that led to Dean's downfall. And Dean eventually set his sights on another role, far less glamorous than occupying the White House: to be the head of the Democratic National Committee (DNC).

The DNC, which promotes Democratic candidates across the country, is a powerful organization. But it's a far cry from being president. Dean, undaunted, announced in early 2005 that he was seeking the organization's chairmanship. Through assiduous campaigning—even in areas off the Democratic Party's radar—and a vow to ensure the Dems ran a "50 State Campaign" in the next presidential election, he won the post and went on to a phenomenally successful tenure that teed up Barack Obama's historic presidential win. Dean never became president, but through his service as DNC chair, he overcame the sting of his loss and found another way to accomplish his goal.

Time Heals All Wounds

In the business sphere, similarly, the key to successful rebranding is consistency and proving your values by living them out every day. You may remember Michael Milken best as the symbol of 1980s Wall Street excess. In 1989, the former Wall Street highflier was charged with securities and reporting violations; he eventually paid a $200 million fine and served just under two years in prison. For many disgraced financiers, that would be the end of the story. But two decades later, Milken has redeemed himself entirely, even earning a 2004 *Fortune* magazine cover story praising him as "The Man Who Changed Medicine." How is that possible?

For one, Milken began his commitment to philanthropy in the 1970s and launched his family foundation in 1982, long before he ran into problems with the government. He's funded a cornucopia of causes, from teacher recognition to inner-city issues, but has notably affected health care, raising hundreds of millions of dollars and driving innovations in treating prostate cancer, melanoma, and more. Said former CNN host Larry King, "When they cure this disease [cancer], they'll have to call it the Milken cure." Milken's commitment to charity is obviously genuine and provides a powerful lesson for all of us. With hard work, focus, and consistency, it's possible to become who you want to be, regardless of your previous brand or even your previous mistakes.

In today's world, reinventing yourself isn't optional. We're constantly learning, growing, and adapting; to be true to ourselves, our personal brands need to reflect that. Taking control of your reputation and making sure it reflects the real you is a critical starting point. Especially in the internet era, traces of your old identity will never completely disappear, and as long as you're thoughtful about what you've learned along the way, that's OK.

The challenge for all of us as we reinvent ourselves (in large ways or small) is to be strategic about identifying how we wish to be perceived, developing a compelling story that explains our evolution, and then spreading that message. Consider it search engine optimization for your life: the more connections you seek out and make, and the more value and content you regularly add to the stream, the more likely it is that your new brand will be known, recognized, and sought out.

REMEMBER:

- ✓ Don't assume your rebranding is a done deal. It's a process, not a onetime activity, so keep monitoring your reputation to ensure you're being perceived by others the way you'd like.

- ✓ If there's a key behavior you need to change (losing weight, asking for more referrals, writing at least one blog post a week), make a public commitment, with penalties attached if you don't succeed. The glare of the spotlight (and the threat of financial loss) can do wonders for your motivation.

- ✓ Reevaluate periodically. Your goals might have seemed great at the time, but if they're making you unhappy now or don't fit where you are at this point in your life, go ahead and reconsider them.

- ✓ Be consistent in your new brand. If you want people to treat the new you as a reality, rather than just a phase, you have to reinforce it over time and demonstrate your steady commitment.

- ✓ Your old brand never goes away. But, if you're thoughtful about the process, your past experiences can add to and enrich your personal brand, even if there have been struggles along the way.

Make Your Reinvention Work

For generations, the establishment mantra has been "work hard and you'll be recognized on the basis of merit." The net result? The guys with connections and powerful patrons got all the breaks. But now, we're in the midst of a new era of faster-moving professional trajectories, shorter tenure at jobs, and the ability to instantly communicate your message across the world. That means your reputation isn't a closely guarded secret, whispered about in corridors anymore. You can monitor and shape how you're perceived in real time and make adjustments as necessary.

That's important if you're committed to building a career at your company, moving up the ranks, and striving for the C-suite. It's even more important if, like many of us, your ambitions evolve over time and you want to change roles, firms, or even professions. People are too busy paying attention to themselves to pay close attention to you. Left to chance, their impression of you will be haphazard, grabbing onto the last thing they heard or a faint impression from years ago. Luck might be with you—or it might not. You owe it to yourself to take a more systematic approach.

It's often hard, though, to see yourself as others do. We all have blind spots, when it comes to both our strengths and our weaknesses. That's why it's so important to start by bringing in trusted friends and colleagues to help you better understand where you're starting and the unique gifts you possess. By talking with them individually and doing 360 interviews or holding a personal focus group, you can glean important insights that you might not otherwise learn. Looking yourself up online and reviewing old performance reviews can also provide a sense of how others may be viewing you from the outside in.

Armed with this information, you can move into research mode. You'll start behind the scenes, with online research and a book binge to ensure you're up on the canonical texts of the industry and can talk a good game when it comes to current trends. Next, through friends or alumni connections, you'll reach out to actual people for informational interviews, which, if done well, can lead to long-term professional relationships, rather than just a hit-and-run coffee.

As you begin to get a clearer sense of which directions make the most sense to you, it's time to test-drive those assumptions. (After all, there's only so much you can learn on paper or through meetings at coffee shops.) Whether you choose to dive in with a full-time internship or apprenticeship, or to test the waters by volunteering on weekends, you'll be experiencing a new job or profession on the ground, making contacts, and evaluating whether it's a good long-term fit.

You'll also start to focus on the skills you need to develop for your next professional identity. In some cases, you can expand the boundaries of your current job to get more experience, or you may be able to moonlight and subsidize your new path by working diligently in your current role. You may also be considering graduate school, which is sometimes mandatory (you're not going to get far with your medical aspirations if you don't have an MD). But before diving six figures into debt, think carefully about the skills or connections you want to cultivate. Are there other (cheaper) ways to do it? Could you take a class, or a summer program, or learn by volunteering? Only you can decide the right way to prepare yourself professionally.

Another key ingredient in your professional advancement is finding the right mentor or mentors, because sometimes you'll want to tap the wisdom of several people or a group, rather than one individual. We talked about the importance of finding a mentor who's looking out for your best interests and wants to help you accomplish your goals, rather than pushing her own agenda. And the secret to getting the most out of the relationship is recognizing that you can't just wait for wisdom to be imparted; you need to create your own learning agenda, express thanks regularly, and make a concerted effort to give back to your mentor, however you can.

Though the corporate world often values similarity (hiring recruits from the same school or promoting executives with the same pedigree), the secret to your success actually centers on your difference. You shouldn't even try to compete head-to-head with the people who have been working their way up in your new arena for the past ten or twenty or thirty years. Instead, focus on what makes you different and unique. What's the skill you possess that no one else does? How can you translate your past experience into your new realm? That will be your calling card and path to advancement.

An important component, of course, is finding a compelling way to tell the story of that difference. Your narrative will engage others and allow them to make sense of your transition. You'll make the connections obvious so they understand you're not swinging wildly from one realm to another or trying to become someone else. Instead, you're strategically applying your existing skills in a new way that adds value.

Reintroducing yourself isn't always easy. People have preexisting ideas about you, and you'll need to catch their attention in order to overturn them. That means demonstrating your new identity with the help of validators, like trusted colleagues who agree to talk you up and highlight your recent successes. And where possible, you'll align yourself with prominent projects or initiatives that allow you to showcase your skills to a wide audience.

Next, you'll concentrate on building a portfolio—both online and off—to demonstrate your abilities. As a knowledge worker, it's sometimes hard to show people what you know and can do. That's why it's so essential to create intellectual property that others will want to read, share, and comment on. Whether it's through a blog, a video blog, or a podcast series, you can find the medium where you're most comfortable. Creating content will allow you to set the tenor of the public debate, meet and interact with the leading lights of your industry, and build a reputation as a thought leader. In the real world, meanwhile, you can similarly brand yourself through taking leadership roles in professional associations and becoming a public speaker at industry events.

Finally, the true secret of professional reinvention is to keep moving forward. That means keeping watch on your reputation by monitoring what's being said about you online and turning periodically to trusted friends for an unvarnished look at how you can continue to improve. Sometimes, there are hard behavioral changes you'll have to make, whether it's quitting smoking or drilling down on business development, and only a public commitment or the threat of financial loss can truly mobilize you. Those are the sacrifices you have to make if you really want to make change stick and accomplish something meaningful.

We've all seen too many examples of broken promises and failed intentions. People will come to respect your new brand and take you seriously when they see your day-in, day-out commitment to crafting a new identity. People make mistakes; it's only human. But working hard, being consistent, and building up goodwill over time will enable your community, and the world, to better understand where you're coming from, and where you hope to go with your life. They may even mobilize to help you get there.

Professional reinvention is almost never a onetime, fix-it-and-you're-done job. Instead, it's a way of life and a way of seeing the world—full of opportunity, open to new possibilities, and awaiting your contribution. I hope this book has been helpful as you consider and begin your reinvention process. Reinventing your personal brand allows you to optimize your life, constantly explore new professional frontiers, and be the person you want to be. Congratulations on taking the next step.

Your Professional Reinvention Self-Assessment

Should you reinvent yourself? If you want to win that promotion, shift into another professional role, join a new company, or change careers, you may need to.

Professional reinvention isn't an overnight process, and it involves getting feedback from others, developing new skills, and manifesting the value you can bring. But you can start by taking a thoughtful look at yourself. Your impressions and ideas are likely to change over time as you progress through *Reinventing You: Define Your Brand, Imagine Your Future*. But for now, you can learn a lot by putting your thoughts and assumptions on paper, and using them as a baseline. Consider it a head start on your future.

Who You Are

My greatest strengths are:

_____

_____

_____

_____

My greatest weaknesses are:

_____

_____

_____

_____

My most marketable skills are:

_____

_____

_____

_____

The most unusual aspects of my background or
experience are:

_____

_____

_____

_____

People often ask me about:

_____

_____

_____

_____

Where You're Going

My current professional objective is:

_____

_____

_____

_____

Or, if you're not sure . . .

Several areas that intrigue me professionally are:

_____

_____

_____

_____

The journals, books, and blogs I can read to learn more about my areas of interest are:

_____

_____

_____

_____

The people I know who are connected to those areas are:

_____

_____

_____

_____

The skills I'll need to reach my professional objective (that
I don't presently have) are:

_____

_____

_____

_____

Possible ways to gain those skills might be (volunteering,
job shadowing, reading, graduate school, etc.):

_____

_____

_____

_____

The people I know who might advise me in this
process are:

_____

_____

_____

_____

Your Competitive Advantage

My skills that are most relevant in my new arena are:

_____

_____

_____

_____

What's unusual about me, compared to people in my new realm:

_____

_____

_____

_____

The reason my background or previous experience adds value in my new arena:

_____

_____

_____

_____

The reason that working in this new realm is actually a continuation of what I've done in the past:

_____

_____

_____

_____

Demonstrating Your Value

A major project or initiative in my new arena that I could get involved in might be:

_____

_____

_____

_____

People often ask me about these topics (which might make good blog posts or podcasts):

_____

_____

_____

_____

Professional associations I can join in my new arena include:

_____

_____

_____

_____

Ways I can leverage social media to showcase my new identity include:

_____

_____

_____

_____

I could approach the following organizations about speaking engagements:

_____

_____

_____

_____

The single most important change I can make, or initiative I could undertake, would be:

_____

_____

_____

_____

Good luck in your professional reinvention process. To learn more, or to access hundreds of free resources—from articles to podcasts to videos—visit www.dorieclark.com and follow me on Twitter (@dorieclark.

Classroom or Book Group Discussion Questions

- What public figures have personal brands that you admire? Why?

- Can you think of public figures who have reinvented themselves professionally? How so?

- What do you think made them successful—or unsuccessful—in their reinvention?

- Have you reinvented yourself professionally? In what way? What was easy, or challenging, about the experience?

- Did you plan out your reinvention in advance? If so, what was the process you followed? How did you determine how to get "from here to there"?

- How did you let others know about your new brand? Did they accept it immediately, or did you need to convince them over time to accept the "new you"?

- Do you think professional reinvention is becoming more common? Why? If so, what are the implications of this change?

- How important do you think social media is for personal branding? Do you use social media in a professional context? If yes, what's your strategy for ensuring it advances your professional reputation?

NOTES

CHAPTER 1

1. Megan Woolhouse, "A Jobs Pinch for the Ages," *Boston Globe*, July 21, 2011.

2. Ronald Brownstein, "Upside Down," *National Journal*, June 9, 2011.

3. Ibid.

4. Irving Rein et al., *High Visibility: Transforming Your Personal and Professional Brand* (New York: McGraw-Hill, 2006).

CHAPTER 2

1. Unless otherwise noted, all quotations come from interviews conducted by the author.

2. Jennifer Preston, "Social Media History Becomes a New Job Hurdle," *New York Times*, July 20, 2011, www.nytimes.com/2011/07/21/technology/social-media-history-becomes-a-new-job-hurdle.html?pagewanted=all.

3. Read my article, "How to Repair a Damaged Online Reputation," at www.dorieclark.com/reputation.

4. Craig Lambert, "The Psyche on Automatic," *Harvard Magazine*, November–December 2010, http://harvardmagazine.com/2010/11/the-psyche-on-automatic?page=0,0.

5. Kevin Lewis, "Liking the Women, but Promoting the Men," *Boston Globe*, July 31, 2011, www.boston.com/bostonglobe/ideas/articles/2011/07/31/uncommon_knowledge/.

CHAPTER 7

1. Read my article, "How to Develop Your Unique Brand," at www.dorieclark.com/uniquebrand.

2. http://sethgodin.com/sg/.

3. Aljean Harmetz, "New Face; Moving Up to 'Pretty' Roles: Jennifer Grey," *New York Times*, August 28, 1987, www.nytimes.com/1987/08/28/movies/new-face-moving-up-to-pretty-roles-jennifer-grey.html?scp=5&sq=jennifer%20grey&st=cse.

4. Ann Kolson, "Fairy Tale Without an Ending," New York Times, August 17, 1997, www.nytimes.com/1997/08/17/movies/fairy-tale-without-an-ending.html:scp=13&sq=jennifer%20grey%20nose&st=cse&pagewanted=2.

Notes

5. "Plastic Surgery of the Stars," New York Post, www
.nypost.com/f/print/pagesix/celebrity_photos/plastic_surgery_before_after_vUlD
H3YaHlqKGkvg0NGQbK.

CHAPTER 8

1. Alex Williams, "Too Much Information? Ignore It," *New York Times*,
November 11, 2007, www.nytimes.com/2007/11/11/fashion/11guru.html?
adxnnl=1&adxnnlx=1317233505-fdV7Vk22aN4KDIeuP/Fpkw.

2. "Tim Ferriss on Tolerable Mediocrity, False Idols, Diversifying Your
Identity, and the Advice He Gives Startups," *Signal vs. Noise*, http://37signals.
com/svn/posts/2734-tim-ferriss-on-tolerable-mediocrity-false-idols-diversifying-
your-identity-and-the-advice-he-gives-startups.

3. Melissa Corliss Delorenzo, "Why Hire a Poet to Help Your Company?"
Her Circle, June 16, 2011, www.hercircleezine.com/2011/06/16/why-hire-a-poet-
to-help-your-company/.

4. Danielle Sacks, "Alex Bogusky Tells All: He Left the World's Hottest
Agency to Find His Soul," *Fast Company*, September 1, 2010, www
.fastcompany.com/node/1676890/print.

5. Richard L. Berke, "The 2000 Campaign: Tactics, Ad Blitz to Start as
Bush and Gore Define Key States," *New York Times*, August 20, 2000,
www.nytimes.com/2000/08/20/us/2000-campaign-tactics-ad-blitz-start-bush-
gore-define-key-states.html?scp=4&sq=Al%20Gore%20Bob%
20Shrum&st=cse.

6. Warren Bennis, with Patricia Ward Biederman, *Still Surprised: A Memoir
of a Life in Leadership* (San Francisco: Jossey-Bass, 2010).

CHAPTER 9

1. The Chip Conley material is adapted from Dorie Clark, "Why You
Should Be an Emotionally Open Leader," Forbes.com, March 31, 2012,
www.forbes.com/sites/dorieclark/2012/03/31/why-you-should-be-an-
emotionally-open-leader/; and Dorie Clark, "How to Be Yourself on Social
Media—Without Freaking Out Your Boss," Forbes.com, August 27, 2012,
www.forbes.com/sites/dorieclark/2012/08/27/how-to-be-yourself-on-social-media-
without-freaking-out-your-boss/.

CHAPTER 10

1. "The Copyblogger Files—Interview with Brian Clark," *TopRank Online
Marketing Blog*, www.toprankblog.com/2009/01/interview-brian-clark-copy-
blogger/.

2. Nate Elliott, "The Easiest Way to a First-Page Ranking on Google,"
Forrester Blogs, January 8, 2009, http://blogs.forrester.com/interactive_marketing/
2009/01/the-easiest-way.html.

3. Read my article, "How to Avoid Social Media Overload," at www.dorieclark.
com/overload.

4. "Write a Guest Post for I Will Teach You to Be Rich," www .iwillteachyoutoberich.com/write-a-guest-post-for-i-will-teach-you-to-be-rich/.

5. Darren Rowse, "If You Had a Gun Against Your Head to Double Your Readership in Two Weeks, What Would You Do?—An Interview with Tim Ferriss," *ProBlogger*, July 25, 2007, www.problogger.net/archives/2007/ 07/25/if-you-had-a-gun-against-your-head-to-double-your-readership-in-two-weeks-what-would-you-do-an-interview-with-tim-ferriss/.

6. B. L. Ochman, "Interview—Seth Godin on How Often to Post to Your Blog," *Advertising Age*, January 12, 2009, http://adage.com/article/digitalnext/ interview-seth-godin-post-blog/133719/.

7. Read my article, "Why Social Media Wastes Leaders' Time," at www .dorieclark.com/wasting-time. (But don't take it as an excuse not to do it!)

8. Chris Brogan, "My Big Speaking Offer," December 24, 2011, www .chrisbrogan.com/my-big-speaking-offer/.

CHAPTER 11

1. Check out Kerry Patterson's excellent book *Change Anything: The New Science of Personal Success* (New York: Business Plus, 2011), which addresses the topic.

2. Project for Excellence in Journalism, www.stateofthemedia.org/ 2010/overview_key_findings.php.

INDEX

Index

Index

Index

Index

Index

ACKNOWLEDGMENTS

I owe deep thanks to many people, without whom *Reinventing You* wouldn't have been possible. First, to Josette Akresh-Gonzales, whose help and persistence enabled me to connect with the team at *Harvard Business Review,* and to Gardiner Morse, who gave the nod to a new writer and greenlighted the blog post, "Reinventing Your Personal Brand," from which this book sprang; and to Karen Dillon, who saw its potential and helped the blog eventually become an HBR magazine piece. My agent Carol Franco and my editors, Jeff Kehoe and Erica Truxler, have been invaluable in shepherding this book through the development process and ensuring it's the very best it can be. And you wouldn't be reading this were it not for the top-notch production efforts of Allison Peter; the marketing magic of Julie Devoll, Nina Nocciolino, Tracy Williams, and John Wynne; my Tufts University intern, Emilia Luna; plus the spot-on cover design by Stephani Finks.

I'm extremely grateful to my interview subjects, who were kind enough to speak with me so that others might learn from their experiences. You are an inspiration.

I want to thank everyone at *Harvard Business Review* for giving me the opportunity to write and share ideas regularly on the HBR.org blog and in the magazine. I'd also like to thank my *Forbes* editors, Fred Allen and Bruce Upbin, who have enabled me to blog about professional reinvention and many other topics.

Acknowledgments

Credit for everything is due to Gail Clark, who is the most loving and caring mother anyone could ask for. I'd also like to recognize Ann Thomas, whose kindness and care helped shape me into the person I am today. And Patty Adelsberger: I miss you. I'm deeply thankful to Hilary Harkness, who provided incomparable support during the writing process, and to Gideon and Harriet, the world's best cats and editors. Please consider adopting a homeless pet today (www .petfinder.com).

ABOUT THE AUTHOR

Dorie Clark is a marketing strategy consultant and frequent contributor to *Harvard Business Review* and *Forbes*. Recognized as a "branding expert" by the Associated Press, Clark consults and speaks for a diverse range of clients, including EMC, Google, the Ford Foundation, Yale University, the Mount Sinai Medical Center, and the National Park Service.

Clark, a former presidential campaign spokeswoman, has taught marketing and communications at Tufts University, Suffolk University, Emerson College, and Smith College Executive Education and has guest lectured at universities including Harvard, Georgetown, and the University of Michigan. She is quoted frequently in the international media, including NPR, the BBC, and *U.S. News & World Report*. She is also a columnist for *Mint,* India's second-largest business newspaper, and the American Management Association's publications.

A former journalist, Clark won two New England Press Association awards for her coverage, respectively, of religion and transportation policy. She is also the director of the documentary film *The Work of 1000,* about the successful cleanup of the Nashua River in Massachusetts and New Hampshire. Clark currently serves as cochair of the Board of Visitors of Fenway Health and is a member of the Board of

Overseers of the Massachusetts Society for the Prevention of Cruelty to Animals.

At age fourteen, Clark entered Mary Baldwin College's Program for the Exceptionally Gifted. At eighteen, she graduated Phi Beta Kappa from Smith College, and two years later received a Master of Theological Studies from Harvard Divinity School. She divides her time between Somerville, Massachusetts, and New York City.

For more information, visit www.dorieclark.com or follow her on Twitter @dorieclark.